# I Will Pray for You

# You

*Breaking Free from Evil Influences*

**Bema D Yeo**

## Disclaimer

This book, I Will Pray for You, is intended for general inspirational and spiritual guidance only. The views and opinions expressed herein are those of the author and do not necessarily reflect the views of Light Books Editions or any of its affiliates. The content is provided "as is" without warranty of any kind, express or implied. Neither the publisher nor the author shall be liable for any loss, damage, or other liability incurred as a result of any individual's use of or reliance on the information presented in this book.

The stories and anecdotes recounted in this book are used to illustrate broader spiritual and life lessons and may be composites or fictionalized for that purpose. Names and identifying details may have been changed to protect the privacy of individuals unless otherwise noted. The practices and advice in this book are not intended as a substitute for professional advice or treatment for specific conditions, and readers should consult a professional or their spiritual advisor before making any decisions based on the content of this book.

## Dedicated

*To those who fear the devil and witchcraft, and who have felt the heavy burden of unseen battles, this book is for you. Your fears and struggles are real, and you are not alone. May these pages provide you with the strength and understanding needed to confront and overcome the darkness that seeks to intimidate and oppress you.*

*To those who are willing to stand firm against the forces of darkness, your courage and determination are a testament to the power of faith. Your resilience in the face of adversity is inspiring. This book aims to equip you with the tools and knowledge necessary to continue your brave stand, to protect yourself and those you love, and to shine a light in the darkest of places.*

*And foremost, to God, whose love and guidance have illuminated the path through every shadow, we dedicate this work. Your unwavering presence and divine protection have been our constant source of hope and strength. May this book serve as a humble reflection of your glory and a guide for others to find their way through the trials of life with your light leading them forward*

**Bema D Yeo**

*"Therefore confess your sins to each other and pray for each other so that you may be healed. The prayer of a righteous person is powerful and effective."*

–- **James 5:16**

# Acknowledgement

The title of this book is not meant to mislead you in any way. I believe that if you are meant to read this book, it will find its way to you. As I wrote this book, I faced numerous spiritual attacks that almost made it impossible to complete. However, the title was not chosen by my own free will. I sought guidance and realized that this title serves as a beacon to divert the dark forces while illuminating the path for those sincerely seeking the face of the Lord, yet unknowingly burdened by spiritual yokes.

If you have found this book, congratulations. There is a message inside meant specifically for you. If you were not intended to read it, you likely wouldn't have come across it, and it would have escaped your notice. May God bless you and lead you to what will bring peace into your life and provide you with the guidance you seek.

The forces of darkness despise having their secrecy exposed, and they will undoubtedly work to conceal their ways once more. However, trust that God will continue to reveal the truth, whether through this book or through someone else. Rest assured that His light will always find a way to shine through the darkness. Believe it or not, the truth will emerge, bringing hope and clarity to those who earnestly seek it. Just trust Him and Pray!!!

# Prologue

*In the stillness of the night, when the world sleeps, there is a battle raging that few are aware of. This is not a battle fought with swords or guns, but a spiritual warfare that infiltrates the very fabric of our lives. It is a war against unseen forces, curses, and the pervasive influence of the devil. Many have felt its sting but have not understood its source or how to defend against it. This book, "I Will Pray for You," is a beacon of hope and a guide for those who seek to understand and overcome these spiritual challenges.*

*Throughout these pages, you will embark on a journey to uncover the reality of spiritual attacks and the insidious ways they can manifest in our personal lives, communities, and even within corporations and governments. You will learn to identify the signs of these attacks and understand the enemy's mission and goals. Knowledge is power, and by understanding the devil's tactics, you can better equip yourself to stand firm against them.*

*But understanding the enemy is only the beginning. Building a strong defense is crucial, and this starts with strengthening your relationship with God. Through prayer, faith, and the teachings of the Bible, you can create a shield of protection around yourself and your loved ones. This book will guide you through effective prayer techniques, the importance of community, and daily practices that safeguard against evil influences.*

*Reclaiming your life from the grip of spiritual attacks is not just about defense; it's about breaking free from curses, reclaiming your prosperity, and closing the doors that the devil may use to infiltrate your life. Practical steps and powerful testimonies will inspire and empower you to live a life full of faith, protection, and victory.*

*"**I Will Pray for You**" is more than a book; it is a lifeline to those struggling in the unseen battles of life. It is a call to vigilance, faith, and the unwavering belief that with God by your side, you can overcome any spiritual attack. As you read, may you find the strength, guidance, and courage to face the enemy and reclaim the abundant life that is rightfully yours. Do not be afraid. If they were truly powerful, they wouldn't hide during the day or fear the light. They are weak, but they use fear as their favorite weapon.*

# Introduction

In a world where the visible often overshadows the invisible, many remain unaware of the spiritual battles that rage around them. This book, "I Will Pray for You," seeks to bring light to the often overlooked but profoundly impactful realities of spiritual attacks, curses, and the influence of the devil. These unseen forces can infiltrate our lives, manifesting in various forms of adversity, fear, and confusion. Yet, within this darkness lies an opportunity for profound personal growth, strengthened faith, and the development of spiritual defenses. At the core of this exploration is the understanding that spiritual attacks are real and can affect anyone, regardless of their walk of life. These attacks can come in many forms, from subtle whispers of doubt and despair to more overt manifestations of misfortune and chaos. Curses, too, play a role in this spiritual warfare, often passed down through generations or invoked through malevolent intent. The devil, as the orchestrator of these attacks, seeks to undermine our faith, disrupt our lives, and distance us from God's love.

However, this book is not just about recognizing the presence of evil; it is also about empowering you to stand firm against it. One of the central messages is the importance of self-reliance in the face of spiritual adversity. Self-reliance, in this context, does not mean facing these challenges alone, but rather, developing a strong inner foundation built on faith, knowledge, and personal conviction. By understanding the nature of spiritual attacks and how they operate, you can better prepare yourself to resist and overcome them. Equally important is nurturing a deep and personal relationship with God. In times of spiritual warfare, it is our connection to God that serves as our most powerful defense. Through prayer, meditation, and the study of scripture, we can draw closer to God, seeking His guidance and protection. This relationship is not only a source of comfort but also a wellspring of strength that fortifies us against the enemy's attacks.

The defense against evil requires a multifaceted approach. Beyond self-reliance and a strong relationship with God, practical steps and strategies are essential. This book provides actionable advice on how to protect yourself from spiritual attacks, break curses, and reclaim your life from the clutches of darkness. From effective prayer techniques to daily practices that foster spiritual health, you will find the tools you need to build a robust defense system.

"I Will Pray for You" is a call to arms for those who wish to reclaim their lives from the influence of evil. It is a guide to understanding the spiritual forces at play, empowering you to take control, and fostering a life of faith and protection. As you journey through these pages, may you find the strength to stand firm, the wisdom to recognize and repel the enemy, and the unwavering belief that with God by your side, no darkness can overcome the light.

# Part 1

---

# Understanding Spiritual Attacks

# <u>Chapter 1</u>: The Reality of Spiritual Warfare

In the hustle and bustle of everyday life, it is easy to overlook the spiritual battles that rage around us. Many people remain unaware of the reality of spiritual warfare, dismissing it as superstition or myth. However, those who have experienced the effects of spiritual attacks know that these battles are very real and can have profound impacts on our lives. Spiritual warfare encompasses the struggles between good and evil, the forces of light and darkness, and the ongoing conflict between the kingdom of God and the realm of the devil. Spiritual warfare can manifest in many forms, from subtle temptations and negative thoughts to more overt attacks like curses, misfortune, and demonic oppression. These attacks aim to weaken our faith, disrupt our peace, and distance us from God's love and protection. Understanding the reality of spiritual warfare is the first step in recognizing and combating these unseen forces. Awareness equips us with the knowledge and tools necessary to defend ourselves and protect our loved ones from spiritual harm.

The Bible provides numerous accounts of spiritual warfare, illustrating the ongoing battle between good and evil. Ephesians 6:12 states, "For our struggle is not against flesh and blood, but against the rulers, against the authorities, against the powers of this dark world and against the spiritual forces of evil in the heavenly realms." This verse highlights the nature of our true enemy and emphasizes the importance of spiritual preparedness. Our adversaries are not human; they are spiritual entities that operate in the shadows, seeking to influence and control. One of the most common forms of spiritual attack is temptation. The devil uses temptation to lure us away from God's path, enticing us with the pleasures of the world. These temptations can lead to sin, which in turn creates a separation between us and God. Overcoming temptation requires vigilance, prayer, and a strong connection to God. By resisting the devil's enticements, we can maintain our spiritual integrity and strengthen our relationship with God. Another significant aspect of spiritual warfare is the presence of curses and negative influences. Curses can be generational, passed down from one family member to another, or they can be invoked through malevolent intent. These curses can bring about illness, financial difficulties, relational strife, and other forms of misfortune. Recognizing the signs of a curse and taking steps to break its hold is crucial for reclaiming one's life and prosperity.

Demonic oppression is another severe manifestation of spiritual warfare. Unlike possession, where a demon takes full control of a person's body, oppression involves external forces that cause distress, anxiety, and torment. People under demonic oppression often experience a sense of hopelessness and despair. Combating this form of spiritual attack requires strong faith, persistent prayer, and often, the support of a community of believers. Spiritual warfare affects communities, organizations, and even nations where the devil seeks to sow discord, division, and chaos wherever he can or want. Corporations also can be influenced by greed and corruption, governments by tyranny and injustice, and societies by moral decay and conflict. Recognizing that these broader patterns of spiritual warfare exist is the starting point to seek God's help in this battle, not only a personal battle but also to work towards the healing and protection of our larger communities. Indeed, despite the formidable nature of spiritual warfare, we are not left defenseless. God has provided us with spiritual armor to protect and equip us for battle. Ephesians 6:13-17 describes the armor of God, including the belt of truth, the breastplate of righteousness, the gospel of peace, the shield of faith, the helmet of salvation, and the sword of the Spirit. Each piece of this armor serves a specific purpose in defending against spiritual attacks and maintaining our spiritual health.

In spiritual warfare, prayer is an incredibly powerful weapon, more potent than we can fully comprehend. Even a simple, two-sentence prayer can have a devastating effect on the forces of evil.

The key lies in praying with genuine faith and righteousness. When our hearts are aligned with God's will and we trust in His power, our prayers become mighty tools that can dismantle the works of darkness and bring forth divine protection and intervention. Through prayer, we can communicate with God, seek His guidance, and ask for His protection. Praying for ourselves and others creates a spiritual shield that can repel the attacks of the enemy. Effective prayer involves more than just words; it requires faith, sincerity, and a heart aligned with God's will. I emphasize the importance of faith because it is the cornerstone of your spiritual journey. When words are spoken with genuine faith, they become powerful instruments of accomplishment. Faith transforms mere words into declarations of divine truth and authority, enabling them to manifest God's will and purpose in your life.

Scripture provides profound wisdom, guidance, and truth that effectively counteract the lies and deceptions of the devil. The Bible is not merely a historical document but a living testament of God's word, offering us the spiritual tools needed to navigate the challenges of life. Through its teachings, we gain clarity, strength, and the ability to discern truth from falsehood, enabling us to stand firm against the enemy's schemes. I understand why some people remain reluctant and skeptical about the word of God. Doubt can stem from various sources, including personal experiences, cultural influences, or the pervasive skepticism of our times. I recall hearing someone claim that the scriptures are not divinely inspired, which made me ponder whether they truly grasp the power of their own words. Such declarations can unwittingly open doors for the devil to work in their lives, binding them with negativity and spiritual vulnerability. It is crucial to recognize the impact of our words and beliefs. When we speak with doubt and disbelief, we create an environment where the enemy can thrive. Conversely, when we embrace and declare the truths found in scripture with faith and conviction, we fortify our spiritual defenses and invite God's blessings into our lives. Understanding the power of scripture and aligning our words with its truth can transform our spiritual journey, providing us with the strength to overcome any challenge the devil may present. By studying and internalizing God's Word, we can arm ourselves with the knowledge needed to resist temptation and stand firm against spiritual attacks. Scriptures such as Psalm 91, which speaks eloquently of God's protection, are especially powerful in times of spiritual distress. These verses offer solace and assurance, reminding us of God's unwavering presence and shielding us from harm. By internalizing and reciting such scriptures, we reinforce our faith and invite divine intervention into our lives, creating a spiritual fortress against the forces of darkness. However, it is essential to understand that prayers are often preventative measures. They serve as spiritual armor, fortifying us against potential attacks. Not everyone, including men of God or priests, possesses the immediate power to rebuke an attack on the spot. Spiritual warfare requires preparedness and ongoing spiritual vigilance, rather than expecting instant deliverance from every assault. Unless someone has tapped into supernatural powers not aligned with God's will, such as voodoo, the process of rebuking spiritual attacks can take time and perseverance. Genuine men and women of God intercede on our behalf, calling upon divine assistance to combat these malevolent forces. While their prayers are powerful and effective, the reality is that we may still experience some of the struggle and pain as part of the spiritual battle. Faith and prayer are not magic wands that instantly erase all challenges but are instead vital components of our spiritual defense strategy. By maintaining a steadfast relationship with God, continuously seeking His guidance, and remaining vigilant in prayer, we build resilience against spiritual attacks. Through this journey, we grow stronger in faith, learning to rely on God's enduring strength and protection, even when faced with adversity.

Community and fellowship also play vital roles in spiritual warfare. Being part of a supportive community of believers offers strength, encouragement, and accountability. Together, we can pray for one another, share our struggles, and provide the essential support needed to overcome spiritual battles. The power of communal prayer is immense, fostering a sense of unity and strength that individual efforts alone cannot always achieve. When we unite in prayer, our collective faith and intentions create a formidable spiritual force, offering protection and encouragement to each member of the community. Isolation can make us more vulnerable to spiritual attacks, as it strips us of the mutual reinforcement and encouragement that comes from being part of a faith community. When we are alone, it is easier for doubt, fear, and temptation to creep in, weakening our defenses. In contrast, a supportive community provides a network of protection and solidarity, where each person's faith contributes to the overall strength of the group. This collective resilience helps shield us from the enemy's attacks and keeps us grounded in our faith. It is lamentable that in modern times, we have often lost the sense of community prayer. While personal prayer is vital and deeply meaningful, there is unparalleled power in coming together as a community to seek God's guidance and intervention. Praying together amplifies our voices and unites our hearts, creating an environment where God's presence is palpably felt. When we gather in prayer, we demonstrate our commitment to one another and to God, fostering a sense of belonging and shared purpose. The beauty of communal prayer lies in its ability to transcend individual efforts. If one person's prayer journey extends over several hours, days, months, or even years, the entire community benefits. This is especially true if that individual has a deep, sincere relationship with God, characterized by love and unwavering faith. Their dedication and spiritual connection can enhance the efficacy of the group's prayers, leading to miraculous outcomes that might not have been possible through isolated efforts. In a community, the spiritual strengths of each member are magnified and shared. The sincerity and fervor of one person's prayers can inspire others, creating a ripple effect of faith and devotion. This interconnectedness means that even if some members are struggling or feeling weak in their faith, the collective strength of the community can uplift and support them. The bonds formed through communal prayer are not only spiritual but also emotional, providing comfort and assurance during difficult times. Moreover, communal prayer fosters a sense of accountability and mutual care. When we pray together, we are reminded of our responsibilities to one another and to God. We are encouraged to live out our faith in tangible ways, supporting and caring for each other beyond the confines of prayer sessions. This holistic approach to faith strengthens the entire community, making it a bastion of spiritual resilience and compassion. Praying together must be a commitment for the greater good not self-interest. The commitment to pray for one another as a community also nurtures a deeper relationship with God. As we intercede on behalf of others, our empathy and compassion grow, aligning our hearts more closely with God's love and intentions. This selflessness in prayer transforms our spiritual lives, drawing us nearer to God's presence and reinforcing our collective bond as His children. the power of community prayer lies in its ability to unite us in faith, purpose, and love. By praying together, we not only fortify our spiritual defenses but also create a supportive, nurturing environment where each member can thrive. The collective strength of our prayers, fueled by genuine relationships with God and each other, becomes an unbreakable shield against the forces of darkness, ensuring that all our prayers are answered in God's perfect timing and way.

## ❖ What is are Spiritual attacks?

Spiritual attacks are assaults on a person's spirit or soul, aimed at weakening their faith, causing distress, and creating obstacles in their spiritual journey. These attacks can come in various forms and can significantly impact a person's mental, emotional, and physical well-being. Unlike physical attacks, spiritual attacks are often subtle and can go unnoticed until they have caused considerable damage. Recognizing and understanding these attacks is crucial for anyone seeking to maintain a strong spiritual foundation. In the Bible, spiritual attacks are frequently mentioned and described. Ephesians 6:12 states, *"For our struggle is not against flesh and blood, but against the rulers, against the authorities, against the powers of this dark world and against the spiritual forces of evil in the heavenly realms."* This passage highlights the nature of our true enemies which are the spiritual entities that operate in the unseen realm. The Bible also provides numerous examples of spiritual attacks, such as the temptation of Jesus in the wilderness (Matthew 4:1-11) and the afflictions faced by Job (Job 1-2). other holy books also acknowledge the reality of spiritual warfare. In the Quran, there are references to the whisperings of Shaitan (Satan) who seeks to lead believers astray. Surah Al-Falaq (113:1-5) and Surah An-Nas (114:1-6) are often recited for protection against such evil influences. These texts highlight the importance of seeking

27

refuge in God and being vigilant against spiritual threats, they are real.

Spiritual attacks can affect various aspects of a person's life, including their relationships, health, career, and overall sense of peace and well-being and by the time you realize, the damages can be huge. For example, a person might suddenly experience unexplained illnesses, constant misfortune, or intense feelings of fear and anxiety. These manifestations can disrupt daily life and hinder one's ability to function effectively. Spiritual attacks can also lead to a sense of isolation, as the person may feel that no one understands their struggles.

One common form of spiritual attack is *temptation*, which seeks to lure individuals away from their faith and moral principles. The devil, as depicted in various religious texts, often uses temptation to plant seeds of doubt, despair, and desire. For example, someone might be tempted to engage in unethical behavior, such as lying or cheating, which can lead to a spiral of guilt and further spiritual attacks. Another form of spiritual attack is oppression, where an individual feels a persistent, overwhelming sense of heaviness or darkness. This can manifest as chronic depression, anxiety, or a sense of hopelessness. Unlike possession, where a person is completely overtaken by a demonic force, oppression is more about external pressures that weigh down the spirit, making it difficult to feel joy or purpose. Curses and hexes are also considered forms of spiritual attacks but, I will discuss furthermore curses in the next section. These are often intentional acts of malevolence directed towards someone to cause harm or misfortune. Such attacks can lead to a series of unfortunate events in a person's life, such as financial ruin, relational breakdowns, or health crises. Recognizing a curse often involves noticing patterns of repeated and unexplained negative occurrences.

To recognize a spiritual attack, it is important to be aware of sudden and unexplained changes in your life and behavior. You might notice a drastic shift in your or someone mood or energy levels, feeling constantly drained or agitated without any apparent reason. Unusual disturbances in sleep, such as persistent nightmares or insomnia, can also be indicators of spiritual attacks. Feelings of extreme isolation and detachment from loved ones can be another sign. Spiritual attacks often aim to isolate the victim, making them feel misunderstood and alone. This isolation can lead to strained relationships and a further sense of despair. Recognizing these signs early can help in seeking the necessary spiritual support and intervention. You can also notice a decline in spiritual practices, such as prayer, meditation, or reading holy scriptures, can be a red flag. Spiritual attacks aim to sever the connection between individuals and their faith. If a person finds themselves increasingly reluctant or unable to engage in these practices, it may indicate that they are under spiritual assault.

Pay attention to your intuition and spiritual discernment. Often, individuals can sense when something is not right, even if they cannot pinpoint the exact cause. Trusting these feelings and seeking guidance from spiritual mentors or leaders can provide clarity and support during such times but, I will provide a prayer that can help you, but you have to trust every word from this prayer and believe (faith). Generally, to response to spiritual attacks, various strategies can be employed. Regular prayer, reading and meditating on holy scriptures, and participating in communal worship can strengthen one's spiritual defenses. Additionally, seeking support from a faith community can provide encouragement and protection, reinforcing the individual's spiritual armor but my favorite is the prayer you do yourself or the help you can get from your mentor. I will discuss the choice of the mentor later or in a different book. Spiritual attacks are real and can have profound effects on various aspects of a person's life. Understanding the nature of these attacks, recognizing the signs, and employing spiritual strategies to combat them are essential steps in maintaining spiritual health and resilience. By staying vigilant and grounded in faith, individuals can protect themselves from these unseen forces and continue to grow spiritually. Now here the prayer, very simple

### *A Prayer to Rebuke Spiritual Attacks*

‣ *Heavenly Father, in the mighty and powerful name of Jesus Christ, I come before You, seeking Your divine intervention and protection. As I face spiritual turmoil, I call upon Your sacred names to shield and deliver me.*

 ‣ *Jehovah Sabaoth (The Lord of Hosts), God of the angelic armies, I ask You to dispatch Your heavenly forces to surround me. Let them form a barrier of protection that no spiritual wickedness can penetrate. Rebuke the forces of darkness that seek to harm me.*

 ‣ *Jehovah Mekoddishkem (The Lord Who Sanctifies You), sanctify me by Your Holy Spirit. Set me apart from the evil that prowls around, seeking to ensnare my soul. Cleanse me with Your holy fire, and let Your light dispel every shadow of darkness in and around me.*

 ‣ *Jehovah Shalom (The Lord Is Peace), I seek Your peace in this storm. Calm my mind and fortify my heart against fear and doubt. Let Your presence envelops me, guarding me in a fortress of peace that withstands all spiritual assaults.*

‣ *Lord, I declare that no weapon formed against me shall prosper, and every tongue that rises against me in judgment You will condemn. I claim victory over the spiritual attack through Your power and might. Protect me, guide me, and lead me into greater light and truth.*

‣ **In Jesus Name, I pray,**

‣ **Amen.**

If you seek to deepen your prayer life, consider exploring the special prayer book titled "Divine Prayers." This exquisite collection offers a diverse array of prayers designed to meet your spiritual needs and enrich your connection with the divine. Each prayer within this book has been carefully crafted to provide comfort, guidance, and inspiration, making it an invaluable resource for anyone looking to enhance their spiritual journey.

## ❖ What are Curses?

Curses are negative spiritual pronouncements or actions intended to bring harm, misfortune, or suffering to individuals or groups. They can stem from malevolent intentions or can be perceived as divine punishments for wrongdoing. Throughout history, curses have been a common theme in various cultures and religious traditions, often viewed as powerful and destructive forces that can affect many aspects of life. Understanding curses involves recognizing their origins, manifestations, and the means to break their hold. In the Bible, curses are mentioned frequently, often as consequences for disobedience to God's commandments. In Deuteronomy 28, blessings and curses are detailed based on the obedience or disobedience of the Israelites. Verses 15-68 outline the curses that will befall those who turn away from God, including disease, famine, and defeat by enemies. These biblical curses serve as warnings and are intended to encourage adherence to divine laws. The story of Cain and Abel in Genesis 4 is a notable biblical case. After Cain kills his brother Abel, God curses Cain, saying, "You are cursed from the ground, which has opened its mouth to receive your brother's blood from your hand" (Genesis 4:11). This curse marks Cain, making him a restless wanderer on the earth, highlighting the severe consequences of his actions.

In the Quran, curses are also addressed and refers to curses as a form of divine retribution for those who reject God's guidance and engage in sinful behavior. The Surah Al-Baqarah (2:159) mentions "Indeed, those who conceal what We sent down of clear proofs and guidance after We made it clear for the people in the Scripture - those are cursed by Allah and cursed by those who curse." This reflects the idea that curses can result from both divine judgment and human actions. Centuries ago till today, some families are experiencing generations of financial hardship and illness despite various efforts to improve their situation, they find themselves repeatedly falling into the same patterns of misfortune. This could be perceived as a generational curse, where the negative effects seem to pass down from one generation to the next, creating a cycle that is hard to break. An individual may constantly face unexplained setbacks in their personal and professional life despite their best efforts, they always encounter obstacles and failures that seem beyond their control. This persistent misfortune could be interpreted as a curse, especially if it follows a pattern of intentional malevolence from others or as a result of past actions.

Recognizing a curse involves identifying patterns of repeated and unexplained negative occurrences. These patterns often defy logical explanations and persist despite efforts to change them. Common signs of a curse include chronic health issues, recurring financial problems, relationship breakdowns, and a pervasive sense of bad luck or misfortune. Intuition and spiritual discernment can also play a role in recognizing a curse, as individuals may sense a lingering negative influence in their lives.

Breaking a curse requires a combination of spiritual, mental, and practical actions. Spiritually, prayer and seeking divine intervention are crucial. Many faith traditions offer specific prayers and rituals designed to break curses and invoke protection. In Christianity, prayers invoking the blood of Jesus and asking for God's deliverance can be powerful tools in breaking curses. Reciting protective scriptures, such as Psalm 91, can also provide spiritual strength and reassurance. At the end of this section, I will provide you a prayer to break curse but remember that confession and repentance are also important steps in breaking a curse if you realize that you have done something and offended somebody particularly if the curse is perceived as a consequence of past actions or sins. Acknowledging and repenting for any wrongdoing can help lift the spiritual weight of a curse. In some cases, seeking forgiveness from those who may have been wronged is also necessary, as it can release the negative energy associated with the curse easily. Practically, taking steps to address the root causes of misfortune is essential. This might involve seeking medical treatment for health issues, financial counseling for money problems, or therapy for relationship difficulties. Combining practical actions with spiritual practices can create a holistic approach to breaking the cycle of a curse.

Engaging with a faith community, participating in group prayers, and seeking counsel from spiritual leaders or mentors can provide strength and encouragement. The collective faith and support of a community can significantly amplify efforts to break a curse, creating a positive and spiritually uplifting environment. The power of communal prayer and shared spiritual practices cannot be underestimated. When individuals come together in faith, their combined spiritual energy can become a formidable force against the powers of darkness and negativity. This is the story of a young man who lived under the weight of a curse, unaware of its existence until he joined a community in prayer. Through the collective prayers and spiritual discernment of the group, God revealed the hidden curse to one of the members. The revelation was startling: in his youth, the young man had committed a grave sin by engaging in an illicit relationship with his father's wife, who was not his biological mother.

This sinful act had cast a long shadow over his life, manifesting as an inability to maintain healthy relationships with women. As he grew older, he found himself repeatedly failing in his romantic endeavors, unable to forge lasting connections. The curse seemed to taint every aspect of his personal life, causing frustration and despair. However, the power of communal prayer and the intervention of a spiritually aware community member brought the truth to light. Recognizing the root cause of his struggles was the first step toward breaking the curse.

With the support of his faith community, the young man embarked on a journey of repentance and spiritual healing. He confessed his sin, sought forgiveness, and prayed fervently for deliverance. The community stood by him, offering prayers, guidance, and unwavering support. This collective effort helped to break the chains of the curse that had bound him for so long. Through the power of faith and community, the young man experienced a profound transformation. The curse that had plagued his relationships was lifted, and he began to heal emotionally and spiritually. He eventually found the strength to build healthy, lasting relationships, free from the shadows of his past. This story illustrates the remarkable impact of communal faith and support in overcoming spiritual burdens. When individuals come together with a shared purpose and faith, they can create a powerful spiritual force capable of breaking curses and fostering positive change. The young man's journey from despair to healing underscores the importance of community in spiritual warfare and personal transformation.

### *A Prayer for Breaking Curses*

‣ *Heavenly Father, Almighty God, in the mighty and powerful name of Jesus Christ, I come before You seeking Your divine intervention. I stand on the promises of Your Word to break any curses that may attempt to bind me or my lineage. In Your mercy and might, hear my prayer.*

‣ *Jehovah Rapha (The Lord That Heals), heal my spirit, soul, and body from any affliction caused by curses. Let Your healing balm restore what has been damaged, and renew me completely in Your love.*

‣ *Jehovah Nissi (The Lord Is My Banner), under Your banner, I seek refuge and victory. May Your banner over me be a sign of Your protection and a declaration of my deliverance from any curse aimed against me.*

‣ *Jehovah Tsidkenu (The Lord Our Righteousness), clothe me in Your righteousness. Let any curse trying to cling to me be repelled by the purity and holiness of Your presence, for in You, I am justified and sanctified.*

‣ *Jehovah Mekoddishkem (The Lord Who Sanctifies You), set me apart from any generational curses or bindings. Sanctify me with Your truth; Your word is truth. Create a clean heart within me and renew a steadfast spirit within me.*

‣ *Jehovah Shalom (The Lord Is Peace), fill my life with Your peace, surpassing all understanding. Let Your peace guard my heart and mind, dispelling any chaos or confusion that curses may attempt to bring.*

*‣ Jehovah Sabaoth (The Lord of Hosts), Lord of the heavenly armies, fight this battle for me. Let Your angelic hosts break down and destroy any demonic strongholds or generational curses that seek to enslave me.*

*‣ Jehovah Jireh (The Lord Will Provide), provide for my every need according to Your riches in glory. Release me from any curse of lack or poverty, and open the windows of heaven to pour out Your blessings upon me and my family.*

*‣ In the powerful name of Jesus, I declare my freedom from curses. By His stripes, I am healed, by His death, I am redeemed, and by His resurrection, I am set free. I claim victory and liberation over any and all curses. **Amen.***

## ❖ Understand Witchcraft

Witchcraft is often perceived as the practice of using supernatural powers or magic to harm, manipulate, or control individuals and events. Historically and culturally, it has been surrounded by fear and misunderstanding, with various interpretations across different societies. While some view it as folklore or superstition, others recognize it as a real and malevolent force that can cause significant harm to individuals and communities. Witchcraft can operate in people's lives in several ways. Practitioners, often referred to as witches or sorcerers, may use spells, charms, incantations, or rituals to invoke supernatural powers. These practices are believed to manipulate natural forces, spirits, or demons to achieve specific outcomes. Common targets of witchcraft include causing illness, financial ruin, relationship breakdowns, and general misfortune.

One of the primary ways witchcraft affects people's lives is through psychological manipulation. The fear of being cursed or bewitched can lead to severe anxiety, stress, and paranoia. This fear can become a self-fulfilling prophecy, where the belief in the curse itself causes mental and emotional distress, which then manifests in various forms of misfortune or ill health. Witchcraft can also have tangible effects on people's physical health. Those who believe they are victims of witchcraft may experience unexplained illnesses, chronic pain, or sudden health deteriorations that defy medical explanation. This can lead to a vicious cycle of seeking multiple medical opinions and treatments without finding relief, exacerbating the victim's physical and psychological suffering.

In the realm of business and professional life, witchcraft can cause significant disruptions. A business owner who believes they are under a spell may experience unexplained financial losses, sudden drops in clientele, or internal conflicts among staff. These issues can hinder business growth and stability, creating an environment of fear and uncertainty. Professional life can also be affected by witchcraft. Individuals may face inexplicable obstacles in their careers, such as being overlooked for promotions, encountering continuous conflicts with colleagues, or dealing with a tarnished reputation without a clear reason. Such experiences can lead to job dissatisfaction, decreased productivity, and even unemployment.

Professional life can also be affected by witchcraft. Individuals may face inexplicable obstacles in their careers, such as being overlooked for promotions, encountering continuous conflicts with colleagues, or dealing with a tarnished reputation without a clear reason. Such experiences can lead to job dissatisfaction, decreased productivity, and even unemployment.

Relationships are another area where witchcraft can have a devastating impact. Marriages and partnerships may suffer from constant arguments, infidelity, or emotional disconnection. Family dynamics can become strained, with unresolved conflicts and a pervasive sense of mistrust and resentment. These relational issues can lead to separations, divorces, and long-term emotional scars. Witchcraft can also infiltrate social networks and communities, creating divisions and fostering a climate of suspicion. Friendships may dissolve due to misunderstandings or unexplained behavior, and community cohesion can be undermined by rumors and accusations of witchcraft. This can result in social isolation for individuals who are perceived to be cursed or practicing witchcraft.

To combat the effects of witchcraft, prayer is a powerful tool. Prayers to neutralize witchcraft should focus on seeking God's protection, guidance, and intervention. A common approach is to use scripture-based prayers, invoking the power of God's word to break any curses or spells. Psalm 91 speaks of God's protection and can be recited regularly to seek divine safeguarding. Effective prayer is to ask for the Holy Spirit's presence and power to break any bonds of witchcraft. Praying for the Holy Spirit to cleanse and sanctify one's home, workplace, and personal life can create a spiritual barrier against any malevolent forces. Additionally, prayers of repentance and forgiveness are crucial, as they can break any legal grounds that witchcraft might have over an individual's life.

It is also beneficial to engage in communal prayers with fellow believers. Collective prayer amplifies spiritual strength and creates a protective shield over individuals and communities. Joining prayer groups, participating in church services, and seeking support from spiritual leaders can provide additional layers of defense against witchcraft. In addition to prayer, practical steps should be taken to protect oneself from witchcraft. This includes removing any objects associated with witchcraft from one's environment, avoiding involvement in occult practices, and staying rooted in a strong spiritual routine of reading scripture, fasting, and worship. Maintaining a close relationship with God through these practices can reinforce one's spiritual armor.

### *Prayer to Combat, Rebuke, and Nullify Witchcraft*

*Heavenly Father, I come before You in the mighty name of Jesus Christ, seeking Your divine intervention in the spiritual battles I face. Your Word declares that You have given us authority to trample on snakes and scorpions and to overcome all the power of the enemy; nothing will harm us. I claim this promise as I confront and rebuke every plan of witchcraft aimed against my life, my family, and my community.*

*Lord, You are my Shield and my Strong Tower. I ask You to dismantle every strategy that the enemy has devised against us. Let every curse, hex, and spell be broken now by the power of Jesus 'name. I declare that every chain of evil intent is shattered, and every plot of malice is overturned. Your light dispels all darkness, and Your truth sets us free. I stand in the authority You have bestowed upon me, and I command peace and order to prevail in my surroundings.*

*Fill me with Your Holy Spirit, that I may remain vigilant and discerning of the enemy's schemes. Strengthen my faith and fortify my spirit with courage and resilience. May I continually dwell under the protection of Your wings, confident in Your power to protect and victorious in Your promise to deliver. Let Your will be done, and Your kingdom come, on earth as it is in heaven.*

**In Jesus name I pray, Amen**

## ❖   How the devil's agents operate?

The concept of the devil's agents encompasses various entities and individuals believed to act on behalf of evil forces, executing plans to undermine faith, spread chaos, and inflict harm. These agents can manifest in both supernatural and human forms, working subtly or overtly to achieve their malevolent goals. They are at all levels of the society, government, corporations, small business, they are everywhere. The devil's agents often operate through deception and lies. They thrive on creating confusion and leading people away from the truth. By twisting facts, spreading falsehoods, and encouraging doubts about fundamental beliefs, they weaken the spiritual resolve of individuals. In the Bible, the devil is referred to as the "father of lies" (John 8:44), highlighting the central role of deceit in his strategies. The deception can manifest in various ways, from misleading thoughts and ideas to deceptive appearances and false teachings.

They exploit human weaknesses and vulnerabilities, and the Devil's agents are adept at identifying and exploiting areas where individuals are most susceptible, such as pride, greed, lust, and fear. By tempting individuals to indulge in sinful behaviors or unethical actions, they create spiritual and moral decay. The temptation of Jesus in the wilderness (Matthew 4:1-11) showcases how the devil targets basic human needs and desires to lead people astray. In terms of discord and division, one of the primary tactics of the devil's agents is to create strife and conflict among people. This can be seen in personal relationships, communities, and even nations. By fostering anger, jealousy, and mistrust, they disrupt harmony and unity, making it easier to spread chaos and weaken collective strength. This division is often subtle, beginning with small misunderstandings and grievances that grow into larger conflicts.

The devil's agents may engage in direct spiritual attacks, such as curses, hexes, or spells intended to harm individuals. These attacks can result in physical illness, mental distress, or unexplained misfortunes. In many cultural and religious contexts, it is believed that certain rituals and practices can summon dark forces to carry out these attacks, further entrenching the victim in a cycle of suffering and despair. They influence positions of power and authority. Devil's agents can infiltrate governments, corporations, and other institutions, manipulating leaders to make decisions that perpetuate injustice, corruption, and oppression. By controlling influential positions, they can have a far-reaching impact on society, perpetuating systems that benefit evil agendas. This influence often manifests in policies and practices that harm vulnerable populations and create widespread suffering. They promote materialism and idolatry. By encouraging the pursuit of wealth, status, and worldly pleasures, devil's agents divert attention away from spiritual growth and divine connection. This focus on materialism leads to a sense of emptiness and dissatisfaction, as true fulfillment can only be found in a relationship with God. Idolatry, whether in the form of worshiping false gods or idolizing material possessions, weakens spiritual resilience and opens individuals to further manipulation.

The devil's agents can easily manipulate emotions and thoughts. They can implant negative and destructive thoughts, such as self-doubt, despair, and hopelessness, which can paralyze an individual's ability to act positively. By fostering negative emotions like anger, resentment, and bitterness, they create an environment where sin and evil can flourish. This mental and emotional manipulation can lead to depression, anxiety, and other mental health issues, further distancing individuals from spiritual well-being. Most of the time, they often target spiritual leaders and faithful believers. By attacking those who are strong in their faith, devil's agents aim to weaken the foundation of spiritual communities. This can involve direct attacks on the character and integrity of spiritual leaders, as well as attempts to sow doubt and confusion among their followers. By undermining these key figures, they can destabilize or control the entire faith of a community, making it more difficult for individuals to find support and guidance in their spiritual journeys.

Always remember that the devil's agents operate through a variety of insidious methods designed to disrupt, deceive, and destroy.

*"The thief comes only to steal and kill and destroy; I have come that they may have life, and have it to the full."*

**___ John 10:10**

# Chapter 2: Identifying the Enemy

The devil, known by various names such as Satan, Lucifer, and the Adversary, is depicted in many religious texts as the embodiment of evil and the chief antagonist to God's purposes. Understanding the devil's mission and goals is crucial for recognizing the spiritual warfare that believers are engaged in. devil's primary mission is to oppose God's plans in our lives, leading humanity away from righteousness and bringing about destruction and chaos. However, God has equipped us with everything we need to navigate these challenges and emerge victorious. *The devil does not waste his efforts on those who are spiritually inactive or indifferent. Instead, he targets those who have a significant purpose in the kingdom of God, the chosen ones who are destined to lead and inspire others.*

*These individuals, marked by their strong faith and potential to advance God's kingdom, become prime targets for the devil's attacks.*

*When a chosen one succumbs to the devil's temptations and strays to the dark side, it is seen as a major victory in the realm of evil.* The forces of darkness celebrate such a downfall as an accomplishment, an achievement that undermines the spiritual strength and morale of the faithful. Those who facilitate or contribute to this fall from grace are often rewarded with increased power or higher ranks within the devil's hierarchy. These rewards serve as incentives for further acts of treachery and corruption, perpetuating a cycle of spiritual warfare aimed at destabilizing God's work on Earth.

Despite these ongoing battles, believers can take comfort in knowing that God's power and grace are far greater than any force the devil can muster. Ephesians 6:11-13 reminds us to "Put on the full armor of God, so that you can take your stand against the devil's schemes. For our struggle is not against flesh and blood, but against the rulers, against the authorities, against the powers of this dark world and against the spiritual forces of evil in the heavenly realms. By staying vigilant in prayer, immersing ourselves in Scripture, and maintaining strong, supportive communities of faith, we can fortify ourselves against the devil's attacks. The path to victory lies in our unwavering commitment to God and our reliance on His strength and guidance. In moments of spiritual warfare, it is essential to *remember that the devil's power is limited and ultimately defeated by Christ's sacrifice and resurrection. The devil may win battles, but the war has already been won by Jesus.* This assurance should embolden us to stand firm, resist temptation, and continue our mission to spread God's love and truth. As we persevere in our faith, we must also support and uplift one another, especially those who are most targeted by the devil's schemes. By fostering a strong sense of community and mutual encouragement, we create an environment where the devil's influence is minimized, and God's presence is magnified. The devil's mission to disrupt God's plans and lead the faithful astray is relentless, but it is not insurmountable. *I know you are wondering why the devil's mission is to disrupt God's plan for us. Why doesn't God take him away and let us live a good life?* Well, I will write a special book on that topic.

One of goal of the devil is to deceive humanity. From the beginning, as seen in the story of Adam and Eve in the Garden of Eden (Genesis 3), the devil uses deception to lead people astray. By twisting God's words and sowing doubt, the devil entices individuals to disobey and rebel against God's commandments. Deception remains a powerful tool in the devil's arsenal, aiming to distort truth and reality, causing confusion and leading people away from the path of righteousness. They will try to disrupt and destroy your relationships with both with God and other people because the key is to isolate you to gain better access to your life. By fostering division, hatred, and mistrust, the devil aims to break the bonds that unite people in faith and love since other people can pray for you or warn you about the danger around you. This is evident in various forms, such as family conflicts, community discord, and even international strife. The devil thrives on conflict and seeks to sow seeds of division wherever possible, weakening the fabric of society and isolating individuals from each other and from God.

Another weapon of the devil is fear, they will instill fear and despair by creating situations that induce fear, anxiety, and hopelessness with the aim to paralyze individuals spiritually and emotionally. This can manifest through personal trials, societal upheavals, or even through spiritual attacks. Fear and despair can lead individuals to lose faith in God's goodness and power, making them more susceptible to the devil's influence and control. When they fail fear, they will use temptation that is a powerful weapon. By exploiting human weaknesses and desires, the devil presents temptations that lead people into actions and behaviors contrary to God's will. This is clearly seen in the temptation of Jesus in the wilderness (Matthew 4:1-11), where the devil attempts to entice Jesus with worldly power and immediate gratification. The devil's goal is to lead people into sin, which creates a separation from

God and entraps them in a cycle of guilt and shame.

Another goal of the devil and the more insidious goals of is to corrupt and pervert what is good. By twisting and distorting what is inherently good and holy, the devil seeks to undermine God's creation and His plans. This can be seen in the corruption of institutions, the perversion of truth, and the misuse of gifts and talents. The devil's mission includes turning blessings into curses and twisting what is meant for good into evil purposes. This insidious strategy seeks to pervert and corrupt every aspect of life, including art, culture, and societal norms. A prime example can be seen in the lyrics of many contemporary songs. Instead of uplifting and inspiring, a significant number of these songs promote themes that glorify the devil, perversity, and immoral behavior.

In today's world, what was once considered immoral is now often celebrated as normal or even desirable. This shift reflects the devil's success in distorting moral values and leading society astray. The impact is profound, as these messages are not only accepted but also enthusiastically embraced by many, further entrenching the influence of darkness. Moreover, this perversion extends into the realms of law and governance. There are instances where laws that should protect and uplift humanity are manipulated or crafted to support unethical practices, simply to maintain power and secure positions. This legislative endorsement of immoral behavior is a clear example of how the devil's influence can infiltrate and corrupt even the most foundational aspects of society. It is essential to recognize these tactics and remain vigilant. By discerning the underlying messages in the media that we consume and the laws that govern us, we can resist the devil's attempts to turn blessings into curses. Staying grounded in our faith and principles allows us to see through these deceptions and uphold the true values of righteousness and integrity.

As believers, we are called to be the light in a world increasingly overshadowed by darkness. This involves not only personal piety but also active engagement in promoting truth, justice, and moral clarity. There should be no room for the devil to promote idolatry and false worship. However, when they succeed by diverting worship away from God and towards false idols whether they be material possessions, power, or even self-worship, the devil undermines true faith and devotion. Idolatry leads individuals away from the true source of life and fulfillment, causing spiritual emptiness and alienation from God. The devil will try to prevent the message of salvation and God's love from reaching those who need it. This can be seen throughout history in the form of religious persecution, censorship, and the suppression of religious freedom. The devil's mission is to keep people in spiritual darkness and ignorance, preventing them from experiencing the transformative power of the Gospel. This is one of the reasons, they will accuse and condemn people with light. In the Bible, Satan is often referred to as the "accuser" (Revelation 12:10). By accusing believers of their sins and failures, the devil seeks to instill feelings of guilt, shame, and unworthiness. This can lead to a sense of spiritual defeat and disconnection from God's grace and forgiveness.

There are some situations where the devil will work to blind the minds of unbelievers. As stated in 2 Corinthians 4:4), "*The god of this age has blinded the minds of unbelievers, so that they cannot see the light of the gospel that displays the glory of Christ, who is the image of God.*" By keeping people in spiritual blindness, the devil prevents them from understanding and accepting the truth of the Gospel, thereby hindering their salvation. It is even easier for the devil to create doubt and disbelief to undermine the foundation of a believer's relationship with God. This can be done through intellectual arguments, life circumstances, or direct spiritual attacks. Weakening faith leads to spiritual stagnation and can ultimately result in a complete turning away from God.

At the government, institutions, and organization, the devil will try to corrupt and control the leaders. By influencing those in positions of power, whether in religious, political, or social spheres; the devil can extend his influence over larger groups of people. Corrupt leaders can propagate evil policies, spread false teachings, and lead others astray, amplifying the devil's impact on society.

In sum, through *deception, division, fear, temptation, corruption, idolatry, hindrance of the Gospel, accusation, blindness, weakening of faith, and control over leaders*, the devil works tirelessly to lead humanity away from God and towards destruction. Recognizing these tactics is crucial for believers to stand firm in their faith and resist the devil's influence. Stay focus on God's word, remain vigilant in prayer, and support faith communities and we can counteract the devil's schemes and live victorious lives in Christ. Amen!!!

# Chapter 3: The Web of Evil

The web of evil is a complex and interwoven network of malevolent forces and influences that work together to spread chaos, destruction, and spiritual corruption. This web is meticulously constructed and maintained by the devil and his agents, including demons, practitioners of witchcraft, and other individuals who consciously or unconsciously serve dark purposes. Each strand of this web represents a different aspect of evil, such as deception, temptation, division, and fear, all working in concert to ensnare and weaken individuals and communities. One of the most insidious aspects of the web of evil is its ability to infiltrate and corrupt various areas of life. This includes personal relationships, professional endeavors, societal structures, and cultural norms. In personal relationships, the web of evil can create misunderstandings, foster mistrust, and incite conflicts, leading to broken families and friendships. Professionally, it can manifest as unethical behavior, workplace conflicts, and financial ruin, undermining careers and businesses. On a societal level, the web of evil exploits systemic issues such as injustice, inequality, and corruption, perpetuating cycles of suffering and oppression.

The web of evil is also adept at exploiting human vulnerabilities and weaknesses. By targeting individuals' fears, desires, and insecurities, the devil's agents can manipulate people into making poor decisions that lead to spiritual and moral decay. As an example, the allure of power, wealth, or forbidden pleasures can tempt individuals to engage in actions that compromise their integrity and distance them from God. *Once entangled in the web of evil, individuals may find it difficult to break free, as each poor decision further entraps them and strengthens the hold of these malevolent forces.* Combating the web of evil requires vigilance, spiritual fortitude, and a strong commitment to righteousness. Recognizing the signs of entrapment, such as recurring misfortunes, unexplained illnesses, or persistent negative thoughts, is the first step toward liberation.

Prayer, scripture, and community support are essential tools in this battle. Stay rooted in faith, seeking God's guidance, and fostering supportive relationships to build a spiritual defense that repels the influence of the web of evil

## ❖ The interconnectedness of the devil's agents

The devil's agents and witchcraft are deeply interconnected, forming a network that perpetuates evil and undermines spiritual well-being. This web of malevolent forces operates in a coordinated manner, creating a complex system that is difficult to detect and dismantle. Understanding this interconnectedness is crucial for recognizing and combating the pervasive influence of these dark forces in our lives. The devil's agents include a range of entities and individuals who are consciously or unconsciously aligned with evil purposes. These agents can be spiritual beings, such as demons, or human individuals who engage in practices that serve the devil's objectives. Witchcraft is one of the primary means through which these agents exert their influence, utilizing spells, curses, and rituals to manipulate and control their targets. Witchcraft itself is a broad term that encompasses various practices aimed at harnessing supernatural powers. These practices often involve invoking spirits, casting spells, and performing rituals designed to achieve specific outcomes. Practitioners of witchcraft, or witches, are often seen as key operatives within the devil's network, using their abilities to further his agenda. Their actions can create a ripple effect, impacting individuals, families, communities, and even entire nations.

The interconnectedness of the devil's agents and witchcraft is evident in the way they collaborate to spread chaos and destruction. A witch may cast a curse on an individual, causing a series of misfortunes and this initial act of witchcraft can attract other malevolent forces, leading to a compounded effect where the person's life becomes increasingly difficult and filled with suffering. Never share your whereabouts with people you suspect to be involved in devilish activities, witchcraft, or black magic. This includes avoiding disclosing your travel plans and not answering their calls while you are traveling. The reason for this caution is that they will often try to locate you and connect with an agent nearby to carry out their harmful intentions. Sometimes, they need physical access to you, which they can achieve through mutual friends or even a spouse who might be entangled in their web. They will investigate and share the information they need to accomplish their mission. You might wonder, at what price do they undertake these actions? The reward for their success is typically a rank or elevation in their occult hierarchy, as many powers in these dark realms are associated with achieving higher ranks. Successfully carrying out their mission, they gain more influence and control within their sinister networks. Therefore, it is crucial to guard your personal information and maintain vigilance. Trust only those who are steadfast in their faith and have demonstrated their integrity. Always seek God's protection and guidance in your interactions, ensuring that you are not inadvertently giving the enemy a foothold. Remember, spiritual discernment is vital in identifying and avoiding those who seek to harm you. Surround yourself with a strong, supportive faith community, and rely on God's wisdom to navigate these treacherous waters. *The devil's agents work together to ensure that the influence of witchcraft is far-reaching and enduring*. One of the key strategies used by these interconnected forces is to exploit human weaknesses and vulnerabilities. By identifying and targeting areas where individuals are most susceptible, such as their fears, desires, and insecurities, the devil's agents and witches can manipulate people into making decisions that lead to spiritual and moral decay. This exploitation often occurs subtly, making it difficult for the affected individuals to recognize that they are under attack. The impact of this interconnected network can be devastating, affecting various aspects of a person's life. In personal relationships, for example, witchcraft can cause misunderstandings, conflicts, and emotional distress. The devil's agents may amplify these issues, leading to broken relationships and a sense of isolation. In professional settings, witchcraft can result in career setbacks, financial losses, and workplace conflicts, furthering the devil's goal of creating chaos and instability.

Communities are also vulnerable to the influence of this malevolent network. Witchcraft can foster distrust and division within a community, weakening its social fabric and making it more susceptible to other forms of spiritual attack. The devil's agents can exploit these divisions, turning community members against one another and hindering collective efforts to resist evil influences. This fragmentation makes it easier for the devil to achieve his overarching objective of spreading darkness and despair. The interconnectedness of the devil's agents and witchcraft extends to broader societal and cultural levels. Media, entertainment, and popular culture can be tools through which these forces disseminate harmful messages and

normalize immoral behavior. The devil's agent are infiltrating the influential sectors to shape public perceptions and attitudes, making it more challenging for individuals to discern truth from falsehood and right from wrong. There are a multitude of signs of the devil and recognizing the signs of this interconnected network is essential and starting point for effective spiritual defense. Symptoms of witchcraft and the devil's influence can include persistent bad luck, unexplained health issues, recurring nightmares, and a pervasive sense of fear or dread. *Remain vigilant and seek spiritual guidance when encountering these signs. Do not be afraid, as fear is one of their most potent weapons. Rest assured that God is with you, and His divine army stands ready to protect you. What is the worst that can happen that you haven't faced yet? Death, certainly, but even that is under God's sovereign control. Once you accept that your life and death are in God's hands, you have no reason to fear. My answer is clear: there is no reason to be afraid.*

Have faith and pray as prayer is a powerful tool in neutralizing the influence of the devil's agents and witchcraft. Praying for protection, guidance, and strength can help individuals fortify their spiritual defenses and break free from the grip of these dark forces. Additionally, engaging in communal prayer and seeking support from a faith community can amplify the effectiveness of these efforts, creating a collective shield against spiritual attacks. Avoid practices and influences that may open doors to these forces, such as participating in occult activities or consuming media that glorifies evil. Surrounding oneself with positive influences, such as supportive relationships, uplifting content, and healthy lifestyle choices, can help create an environment that is resistant to spiritual attacks. The interconnectedness of the devil's agents and witchcraft is a formidable challenge, *but it is not insurmountable*. Now let's discuss how these forces operate and communicate to give you an idea.

## ❖ How the Devil's Agents Communicate, Especially Throughout Witchcraft?

The communication methods of the devil's agents, particularly those involved in witchcraft, are sophisticated and often shrouded in secrecy. These agents operate through a variety of channels, employing both ancient practices and modern technologies to coordinate their efforts and maintain their influence.

Traditional witchcraft relies heavily on rituals and ceremonies to communicate with the spiritual realm. *Practitioners often use specific incantations, symbols, and artifacts to summon spirits and demons, seeking guidance, power, and the ability to influence events or individuals*. These rituals are performed in secret, often at *night or in secluded locations, to avoid detection* and to tap into the perceived power of darkness. The secrecy and specificity of these rituals ensure that only those initiated into the practices can understand and execute them effectively. Another key aspect of communication among the devil's agents is the use of coded language and symbols. Witches and other practitioners may use symbols in their spells and curses that hold particular meanings within their circles. These symbols can be inscribed on objects, drawn in specific patterns, or incorporated into various forms of media. Coded language allows these agents to pass messages and instructions discreetly, ensuring that their plans remain hidden from those not involved in their dark practices.

In the modern era, technology has provided new avenues for communication among the devil's agents. Encrypted messaging apps, secret online forums, and dark web communities have become popular platforms for witches and other malevolent actors to share knowledge, plan actions, and recruit new members. These digital spaces offer a degree of anonymity and security, making it difficult for outsiders to infiltrate or monitor their activities. The use of technology allows for a global network of evil practitioners to coordinate their efforts more efficiently than ever before. It may be hard to believe, but some of these individuals even have phone numbers they use to communicate with certain spirits. These spirits, incredibly, provide warnings about situations that might adversely affect the practitioners, ensuring their plans and actions remain effective and unimpeded. I am sure some of you will be astonished or even claim this is a lie. However, it is crucial to understand that the very people who will vehemently oppose this book are likely to be the devil's agents themselves, striving to guard their secrecy. Others who will fight against this book may be those under the yoke of the devil, manipulated into rejecting the truth it contains. I am not inventing anything here, the advent of technology has not only enhanced the connectivity among these malevolent forces but also fortified their ability to operate covertly. Encrypted messages, secret online forums, and dark web communities have become the digital equivalents of ancient covens, allowing practitioners to share knowledge, plan actions, and recruit new members without fear of exposure. This modern twist on ancient practices makes their operations even more insidious and pervasive. In another book I will collect some stories or even my experience that I lived in more details only if God inspired me to do so. Without God's guidance, writing this book could be fatal for me, as the devil's agents hate people talking about or revealing the way they operate, since it could save lives. A full discussion about 'How the Devil's Agents Communicate' could make this book a bit longer, but I aim to be explicit and concise in everything I discuss here. So, let's continue moving forward with our discussion on the means of communication.

Dreams and visions are another means by which the devil's agents communicate, particularly within the realm of witchcraft. The demons and spirits can enter a person's dreams to deliver messages, offer guidance, or sow seeds of fear and doubt. Practitioners of witchcraft often interpret these dreams as divine instructions, using them to guide their actions and decisions. This form of communication is highly personal and can be difficult to discern, as it blurs the line between reality and the spiritual realm. Also sacrifices and offerings are integral to the communication methods of witchcraft. Practitioners may offer animals, objects, or even human sacrifices to appease spirits and demons, seeking their favor and assistance. These offerings are often accompanied by specific rituals and prayers, designed to establish a connection with the supernatural entities being invoked. The nature and significance of these sacrifices vary widely, depending on the cultural and religious context of the practitioners.

Telepathic communication and spirit possession are also some methods used by the devil's agents. Some witches claim to have the ability to communicate telepathically with demons or other practitioners, receiving instructions or sharing information without the need for spoken words. I experienced that more than when God open my ears to listen to what a friend was doing. Spirit possession involves a demon or spirit taking control of a person's body, using it as a vessel to communicate and act. This form of communication is particularly sinister, as it can lead to severe psychological and physical harm for the possessed individual. Divination practices, such as tarot card reading, crystal ball gazing, and astrology, are additional tools used by witches to receive messages from the spiritual realm. These methods are believed to reveal hidden knowledge, predict future events, and offer insights into the lives and intentions of others. With the interpretation of the signs and symbols revealed through divination, practitioners of witchcraft can make informed decisions and carry out their plans with greater precision. I am sure that you are very surprised but, the devil's agents use divination. In sum, traditional rituals, coded language, modern technology, dreams, sacrifices, telepathy, spirit possession, and divination are the methods allow for a coordinated and clandestine network of malevolent forces to operate effectively, spreading their influence and executing their dark agendas.

❖ **How Do You Communicate with the Devil's Agent?**

Communicating with the devil's agents to deter their actions and activities is a nuanced process that requires spiritual discernment, courage, and a deep connection with God. This type of communication is not about engaging in dialogue or negotiations with evil forces but rather about asserting spiritual authority and seeking divine intervention to neutralize their influence. Prayer is the most powerful tool available to communicate with and combat the devil's agents. Through prayer, believers can call upon God's protection and guidance, asking for the strength to resist temptations and the wisdom to recognize the signs of evil. Prayers of intercession, where one prays on behalf of others, are also vital in protecting loved ones and communities from spiritual attacks. Specific prayers, such as the Lord's Prayer, Psalms, and prayers invoking the blood of Jesus, are particularly effective in asserting spiritual authority. The use of Scripture is crucial in deterring the actions of the devil's agents. The Bible is filled with passages that declare God's sovereignty and power over all evil forces. By speaking these Scriptures aloud, believers can affirm their faith and remind themselves of God's promises. Verses like Ephesians 6:11-12, which speak of the armor of God, and James 4:7, which encourages believers to resist the devil, serve as powerful declarations of faith and resistance. Another important aspect is the practice of spiritual warfare. This involves recognizing that there is a spiritual battle taking place and actively engaging in practices that fortify one's spiritual defenses. Fasting, along with prayer, is a powerful combination that can break the strongholds of the devil. During times of fasting, believers deny their physical needs to focus on spiritual growth, seeking God's intervention against the activities of the devil's agents. Also, seeking the Holy Spirit's guidance, believers can gain insight into the nature of the attacks they face and the most effective ways to counter them. The Holy Spirit can reveal hidden truths, expose the tactics of the devil's agents, and provide the wisdom needed to navigate spiritual challenges. Developing a close relationship with the Holy Spirit through prayer and meditation is vital for effective spiritual warfare. Remember the devil's agents thrive on exploiting your weaknesses and vulnerabilities. By living a life that aligns with God's commandments and values, believers can minimize the opportunities for these forces to gain a foothold. Regular self-examination, repentance, and a commitment to ethical behavior are essential in maintaining spiritual strength and resilience.

The final form of communication I want to share with you might surprise you, but it is highly effective. Begin by covering yourself with the blood of Jesus, invoking divine protection and cleansing. Then, invite the presence of the Holy Spirit into your space, welcoming His guidance and power. Approach this communication as if you were speaking directly to the spiritual presence before you. Openly express your grief, concerns, and any other emotions or thoughts you wish to convey. Believe or not they are always listening when you talk to them no matter how far they are and who ever is using that spirit will get your message. This personal and direct form of communication taps into the profound power of faith and spiritual connection. By invoking the blood of Jesus, you are asserting His victory over evil and seeking His protective embrace. This act not only shields you from malevolent forces but also empowers you to stand firm in your faith. Invoking the Holy Spirit further strengthens this connection, as the Spirit is a divine advocate and guide. His presence brings clarity, comfort, and insight, helping you navigate through spiritual and emotional challenges. Speaking to the Holy Spirit as you would to a trusted friend or confidant fosters a deep, intimate relationship that can provide immense solace and strength.

# Part 2

# Building a Strong Defense

# Chapter 4: Strengthening Your Relationship with God

Strengthening your relationship with God is more than a self-rewarding journey that requires intentionality, commitment, and a heartfelt desire to grow closer to the Divine. This spiritual bond is foundational to living a fulfilled and purpose-driven life. Here are several key practices to deepen and enrich your relationship with God. You need to understand that prayer is the cornerstone of any strong relationship with God. It is through prayer that we communicate with Him, share our thoughts, fears, joys, and seek His guidance. Consistent and heartfelt prayer cultivates intimacy with God. It's important to set aside dedicated time each day for prayer, aiming for at least three times daily, to create a sacred space where you can connect with God without distractions. This practice fosters a deeper and more consistent relationship with the Divine, allowing you to seek guidance, express gratitude, and find solace in His presence. Observing the discipline of regular prayer can be highly beneficial, as seen in the example of Muslims who pray five times a day. This routine demonstrates a commendable commitment to spiritual devotion. However, it's important that prayer remains a joyful and willing act of worship rather than a burdensome obligation. Many Muslims seem to struggle with the early morning prayer or feel pressured by societal expectations, leading to a sense of duty rather than delight in their spiritual practice. From my observations and personal experiences, I've noticed that some individuals approach their prayer times with a sense of reluctance or fatigue, particularly during early morning prayers. This can turn what should be a meaningful connection with God into a chore. It's crucial to cultivate a mindset that embraces prayer as a cherished opportunity to communicate with the Divine, rather than a task to be checked off a list. To truly benefit from the practice of regular prayer, one should focus on the intention and attitude behind it. Approach prayer with a heart full of gratitude and anticipation, viewing it as a moment of peace and divine communion. Find joy in these sacred moments, knowing that you are nurturing your soul and deepening your relationship with God. Creating a personal and loving connection with God in prayer can transform this practice from a mere routine into a profound and fulfilling spiritual journey. Additionally, for believers, incorporating different types of prayer - adoration, confession, thanksgiving, and supplication - ensures a well-rounded and robust prayer life.

Reading and meditating on the Scriptures should be a habit as the Bible is God's Word, offering wisdom, guidance, and insights into His character and will. Regular study of the Scriptures not only enhances your understanding of God's teachings but also allows you to hear His voice and align your life with His principles. Meditating on verses that resonate with you can provide comfort and clarity, helping you internalize God's messages and apply them to your daily life. However, it is essential to recognize that the Bible is not just an ordinary book. It is a divine text filled with wisdom and guidance. When reading the Bible, ask God for guidance and be attentive to what you are reading; there is always a message waiting for you. Pay close attention to the Word, and when a particular verse catches your attention, meditate on it and consider praying with that verse. You may be surprised at the insights and peace that come from this practice. Unlike seeking answers from card readers or divination, turning to the Bible provides divine truth and guidance. When you face troubles or questions, gently open your Bible and read the verses from the opened page. In most cases, you will find the answers you seek but, it is all about approaching with faith and an open heart. The Bible serves as a direct line of communication with God, offering timeless wisdom and guidance for every situation. Engaging deeply with Scripture, you allow God's voice to speak into your life. This practice not only provides answers but also strengthens your relationship with the Divine, fostering a sense of trust and reliance on His Word. Remember, the key to receiving the full benefit of reading the Bible is faith. Approach the Scriptures with an open heart and a prayerful mind, trusting that God will reveal what you need to know. I will provide a prayer at the end of this chapter to help you uncovers anything in your life.

Engaging in worship is another powerful way to strengthen your relationship with God. Worship can take many forms, including singing, playing music, dancing, or simply being still in His presence. Worshiping God acknowledges His greatness and sovereignty, allowing you to express your love and reverence for Him. Participating in communal worship, such as church services or prayer groups, can be incredibly enriching, offering opportunities to learn, grow, and support one another in faith. However, it is crucial to seek God's guidance before joining any group. Not all communities may be rooted in true devotion, and some may even be founded on deceptive or malevolent principles.

In today's world, it is disheartening to note that some churches and religious groups may be more focused on numbers and appearances rather than genuinely fostering spiritual growth and understanding the Word of God. *The true measure of a church's value lies not in its size or grandeur but in its commitment to teaching and living by God's Word, and the positive impact it has on its members.* It is important to discern the spiritual foundation of any group you consider joining. Look for signs of true devotion to God, such as a genuine commitment to biblical teachings, an emphasis on spiritual growth, and a community that practices love, compassion, and humility. Avoid groups that prioritize material success or membership numbers over the spiritual well-being of their members. Remember, *the people are the church, not the building, and you do not owe a church a dime from your paycheck.* I know in Malachi 3:9-10 God said:

*"You are under a curse - your whole nation - because you are robbing me."* **Malachi 3:9**

*"Bring the whole tithe into the storehouse, that there may be food in my house. Test me in this," says the Lord Almighty, "and see if I will not throw open*

*the floodgates of heaven and pour out so much blessing that there will not be room enough to store it.*" **Malachi 3:10**

This does not mean that a member has to be forced to pay the tithe or the church has to know how much he is making prior becoming a member. *It has to be a free will, teach your members and let them have the choice to test God.* When they are indirectly forced, the tithe does not work in their favor, it is just a simple transaction. I heard some churches are even getting the direct deposit from the employers just to control how much the member should pay. It doesn't seem right, but if you are comfortable with that, it is your choice. This book is not meant to revolt you but to open your mind about why nothing works for you, even when you are paying your tithe. Do not blame God but yourself; you must understand the scripture. Do not solely rely on what people are saying in the media or elsewhere. God loves everybody, and the true church is a community of believers who gather in the name of Jesus Christ to worship, learn, and support one another in their faith journeys. Church is not a place where designated seats are reserved for members who contribute more financially, nor is it a venue for showcasing the most expensive blazers, dresses, colognes, or jewelry. Remember, your body is no different from anyone else's. Contributing more than others does not guarantee your place in heaven. What truly matters is the state of your heart–your genuine devotion to God. This devotion should be reflected in humility and respect towards others, regardless of their contributions. Earthly wealth and possessions are fleeting. You cannot take your money with you when you pass away. A grave, no matter how elaborately constructed, remains a grave. The money and possessions you leave behind can often lead to discord and conflict among your family members. Without proper foresight and spiritual grounding, these assets can become sources of strife and even violence.

*Instead, prioritize putting God first in your life. Trust Him to guide and protect your resources. By doing so, you ensure that your wealth will be managed wisely and will serve your family well after you are gone. There will be a divine power behind every dime, ensuring that it is used for the good of those you leave behind.*

True devotion to God is not measured by the outward displays of wealth or status but by the inner quality of your heart. Practice humility, show respect to others regardless of their social or financial status, and remember that it is your sincere faith and love for God that truly matter. This is the foundation of a life well-lived and a legacy that will bless your family long after you are gone. How do you want to be remembered? Seeking God's guidance and using discernment, you can find a faith community that will help you grow closer to Him and live out His teachings in your daily life.

Obedience to God's commandments is a tangible expression of your faith and love for Him. Living according to His will involves making choices that reflect His teachings and values. This might mean standing firm in your beliefs, even when it is difficult or unpopular. By choosing to obey God, you demonstrate your trust in His wisdom and deepen your relationship with Him. Obedience is not about perfection but about striving to live a life that honors God and reflects His love. People often tend to use the Bible to their advantage, selectively quoting verses that support their views or justify their actions. However, the true essence of the Bible is not to be used as a tool for self-justification but as a guide for personal growth and transformation. The verses that challenge us, the ones that call us to change or adjust our behaviors, are just as important as those that comfort and affirm us. To fully embrace the teachings of the Bible, we must be willing to accept its guidance even when it points out our flaws and shortcomings. This requires humility and an open heart, recognizing that God's Word is meant to refine us, not simply affirm our existing beliefs and actions. The Bible is a mirror that reflects both our strengths and weaknesses, encouraging us to strive for a higher standard of living. *True spiritual growth comes from allowing the Scriptures to challenge and change us. When a verse convicts us or calls us to alter our ways, we should not resist or reinterpret it to suit our preferences. Instead, we should embrace these moments as opportunities for personal and spiritual development, trusting that God's wisdom surpasses our own.*

Approach the Bible with a willingness to be transformed, we align ourselves more closely with God's will. This journey of continuous self-improvement and alignment with divine principles is the true path to spiritual maturity. It is through this process that we become better individuals, capable of living out the full potential of our faith in every aspect of our lives.

Service to others is another way to draw closer to God. Jesus taught that loving and serving others is a fundamental aspect of our faith. Helping those in need, showing kindness, and practicing compassion embody the love of Christ and fulfill His command to love your neighbor. However, it is essential that helping others comes from a place of free will and genuine love, rather than out of obligation or the desire to please others. The true joy of helping lies in the love and joy you put into every action and the happiness you feel while doing it. When you feel tired or overwhelmed, it's important to take a step back and allow others to continue the work. Forcing yourself to help to the point of exhaustion or harming yourself is not what God desires. God wants you to enjoy every moment you spend helping others and to take care of yourself as well. You can only effectively help others when you are healthy and well. Overextending yourself to please others or to be recognized is not the path God intends for you. Human beings can be hypocritical and fickle, quickly replacing you if you fall. Often, only a few, if any, will check on you to see if you are recovering. People might criticize you whether you work hard or appear lazy. But remember, your goal is to seek God's reward, not human approval. People may not appreciate you as they should, and they might lie to please you or devalue your efforts. Keep in mind that your good deeds are significant, and your motivation should be to serve God, not to receive praise from others. Do not expect a reward from God in a transactional sense; instead, trust in His divine plan. God's rewards often surpass our expectations. While you might be asking for something as simple as healing from a disease, God might have a grander plan for you, extending your days on earth and filling them with happiness and joy. God's plan is always the best, and His rewards are beyond our imagination, encompassing not just the fulfillment of our immediate needs but an abundance of blessings that enrich our lives profoundly.

Develop a habit of gratitude, thanking God for His blessings, both big and small, shifts your focus from your problems to His goodness. Gratitude fosters a positive outlook and strengthens your faith, reminding you of God's constant presence and provision. Keeping a gratitude journal can be a helpful practice, allowing you to reflect on God's faithfulness and build a deeper appreciation for His work in your life. You can also fast as fasting is a spiritual discipline that can enhance your relationship with God by helping you focus on your spiritual needs over physical ones. Fasting creates an opportunity for deeper reflection, prayer, and communion with God. It is a way of expressing your dependence on Him and seeking His guidance with greater clarity. During a fast, the time that would normally be spent eating can be used for prayer and reading the Scriptures, making the experience spiritually enriching. Fasting should be a personal, heartfelt practice, not something done out of obligation or for show. Ideally, those around you should not even realize that you are fasting. Maintain a cheerful demeanor, continue working diligently as you normally would, and avoid drawing attention to your fast. It's important not to use fasting as an excuse to shirk responsibilities or avoid work. The true essence of fasting is to give the best of yourself in service and devotion, enhancing your spiritual journey. Your efforts should be genuine and discreet. If a coworker wants to discuss something or make jokes that might distract you, find a polite way to steer the conversation or simply listen without engaging, if avoiding it altogether isn't possible. Fasting should be a means to become a better person, fostering positive changes in behavior and deepening your relationship with

God. It's a time for self-reflection, repentance, and spiritual growth. Approach fasting with sincerity and humility, focusing on your inner transformation rather than external acknowledgment. Let fasting be a time when you draw closer to God, seeking His guidance and strength. Remember to keep your fast private and maintaining your regular duties, you honor the true spirit of this practice. Remember, the goal of fasting is not only to abstain from food but to nourish your soul, build resilience, and cultivate a deeper, more meaningful connection with God.

### *Prayer for God to reveal hidden things*

*Heavenly Father, You promised in Jeremiah 33:3, "Call to me and I will answer you and tell you great and unsearchable things you do not know." I come to You today, seeking the depths of Your wisdom. Please reveal to me the hidden aspects of my life and the paths You desire me to walk.*

*Lord, as I navigate through the complexities of my daily life, guide me to understand the mysteries and the unseen opportunities You have placed before me.*

*Illuminate my decisions and relationships and unveil anything that is obscured by my limited human perspective.*

*Gracious God, empower me with Your Spirit to discern the revelations You provide. Help me to not only see but also to understand and act upon the truths You unveil. I trust in Your guidance and Your perfect will for my life, knowing that Your plans for me are for my good and Your glory.*

*In Jesus Name, I pray*

*Amen*

# Chapter 5: Utilizing the Word of God

The Word of God, as revealed in the Scriptures, is a powerful tool for spiritual growth, guidance, and defense against spiritual attacks. To fully harness its essence and power, it's crucial to approach the Bible with reverence, intentionality, and a desire to internalize its teachings. Approach the Bible with a heart of prayer. Before reading, ask God for wisdom and understanding to discern His messages. Prayer opens your mind and spirit, allowing you to receive deeper insights from the Scriptures. This practice not only helps in comprehending the text but also in applying its principles to your life. Remember, the Bible is not just a historical document; it is a living word meant to guide and transform. Consistent study and meditation on the Scriptures are key. Set aside regular time each day to read and reflect on the Bible. This discipline ensures that you are continuously feeding your spirit with divine truths. Meditating on specific verses that resonate with you can help internalize God's messages. Reflect on their meaning and relevance to your life and consider how they can shape your actions and attitudes. Memorization of Scripture is another effective way to utilize the Word of God. By memorizing, you can recall God's promises and instructions in times of need. This practice strengthens your spiritual foundation and equips you with ready responses to life's challenges. Verses like Philippians 4:13, "I can do all this through him who gives me strength," can provide comfort and encouragement when faced with difficulties. Applying the Scriptures to your daily life is essential. The Bible offers practical wisdom for every aspect of living, from relationships and work to personal conduct and decision-making. Actively seek ways to implement biblical principles in your actions and decisions. This application demonstrates your commitment to living out God's Word and allows its power to manifest in tangible ways.

Sharing the Word with others is also a vital aspect of effectively using the Scriptures as it helps you memorizing the word. When you learn an important part of the Bible and you think that it will be beneficial to others then share with them. The more you share the faster you memorize and the better you will understand the verse and even make some correction of any misunderstanding. Discussing biblical insights with friends, family, or in study groups can deepen your understanding and foster a sense of community. Teaching and encouraging others with the Word of God not only reinforces your own knowledge but also spreads its transformative power to those around you. Using the Word of God in prayer enhances its power. Pray the Scriptures, incorporating specific verses into your prayers to align your requests with God's promises. This practice not only reinforces your faith but also ensures that your prayers are grounded in biblical truth. Praying Psalm 23 can bring comfort and assurance of God's guidance and provision. Here is a prayer with Psaume 23.

## *Prayer to bring comfort and assurance of God's guidance and provision*

*Heavenly Father, as I reflect on Psalm 23, I find comfort in Your promise of guidance and provision. "The Lord is my shepherd; I lack nothing. He makes me lie down in green pastures. He leads me beside still waters. He restores my soul." Thank You for being my shepherd, meeting all my needs, and bringing peace and restoration to my soul.*

*Even when I face dark and challenging times, I trust in Your constant presence. "Even though I walk through the valley of the shadow of death, I will fear no evil, for You are with me; Your rod and Your staff, they comfort me." I draw strength from knowing You are always by my side, protecting and guiding me. Your goodness and mercy follow me all the days of my life, and I find assurance in Your everlasting care. Amen.*

Engaging with the Bible through various resources can also enrich your study. Commentaries, devotionals, and Bible study guides offer additional perspectives and insights that can deepen your understanding. Listening to sermons or participating in online Bible studies can greatly expand your knowledge and provide fresh insights into how to apply the Scriptures to your life. However, it is crucial to exercise discernment with the teachings of modern-day preachers. Some may lead you astray or create a sense of guilt for their own benefit, positioning themselves as indispensable intermediaries between you and God. These preachers might claim to have extraordinary powers and present themselves as the ultimate saviors, drawing attention away from God, the true source of all blessings. Remember, only God can provide and sustain, not any human. While it is beneficial to pray with others and seek guidance, God sees your heart and sincerity before responding to your needs. It is not the preacher's power that brings about change but your genuine faith and connection with God. When praying or seeking divine intervention, it's important to know that God listens to your heartfelt prayers. You may not always know the exact words or verses to use, but your sincerity and earnest seeking are what matter most to God. Preachers can guide you and help you understand how to communicate with God effectively, but it is ultimately your personal relationship with Him that counts. Trust in God's grace and let your faith be rooted in His unchanging nature, rather than in the abilities of any human leader. It is vital to remember that no pastor, no matter how charismatic or seemingly powerful, can take the place of God. Only God has the power to do all things.

Do not fall into the trap of believing that your pastor is a deity capable of solving all your problems. While a pastor can guide you in your spiritual journey, only God has the omnipotence to truly answer prayers and perform miracles. Be wary of those who claim instant answers to your prayers, especially if these solutions come with strings attached or lead to further complications. If a pastor claims to have the power to heal or provide immediate solutions through means that seem miraculous, consider the source of this power. Genuine miracles come from God and align with His love and grace, without causing further harm or creating dependency. However, if these so-called miracles lead to new problems, requiring continuous visits to the pastor for resolution, it might be a sign of manipulation rather than divine intervention. When God solves your problems, they don't return; when He closes a door, no one can open it, and when He opens a door, no one can close it. God's solutions are complete and perfect, not partial or temporary fixes that lead to further complications. God will never solve one problem only to create another. This is why His answers may sometimes take a little longer. He ensures that everything is addressed thoroughly, with the least harm to others. God's wisdom is perfect, and He orchestrates solutions that do not cause undue harm to others, including the innocent. His timing reflects His comprehensive understanding and deep love for all His creation. Remember, God loves everyone deeply. If He didn't care for you, you wouldn't be here, reading this book and seeking to understand His ways better. His love is inclusive and far-reaching, extending to every person regardless of their circumstances. Trust in His process and His timing, knowing that His plans are always for your ultimate good and the good of those around you. Consider this as an example you praying for a promotion because you have been diligently working at your company for five years and feel entitled to advance. However, God sees the bigger picture. If He grants that promotion immediately, it might mean displacing someone else whose position you covet, a person upon whom many others depend. Instead of causing upheaval, God might inspire the company's leadership to create a new position that aligns with your skills and contributions or to promote the other person to an even better position, making room for your advancement. However, this process requires planning, such as allocating the necessary budget to support the new position. This, in turn, might necessitate attracting new customers or partners to generate additional revenue. God orchestrates all these elements behind the scenes, ensuring that when the promotion comes, it is beneficial for everyone involved. This might involve prompting the company to secure new contracts or business opportunities to fund the new positions. His timing allows for the smooth transition and growth of all parties without causing harm or resentment. Always trust in God's perfect timing and comprehensive plan then you can be assured that the promotion, when it comes, will not only be right for you but also harmonious for everyone affected. This divine orchestration underscores the depth of God's wisdom and love, ensuring that His blessings are complete and bring peace and prosperity to all involved. This is just one example among many, but if it is the devil you are asking for a promotion, the results may come quickly, but the negative consequences can be enormous. Trust me, the Bible is clear about the dangers of such shortcuts. As it says in **2 Thessalonians 1:6-7** *"God is just: He will pay back trouble to those who trouble you and give relief to you who are troubled, and to us as well. This will happen when the Lord Jesus is revealed from heaven in blazing fire with His powerful angels.*"

Relying on God's timing and process ensures that your blessings come without hidden pitfalls or destructive outcomes. While the devil may offer quick fixes, they often come with significant and detrimental costs. God's approach, though it may require patience, brings true and lasting rewards that benefit not only you but also those around you. Trust in God's plan, and you will align yourself with His justice and mercy, receiving blessings that are pure and beneficial. Patience in His process protects you from the deceitful traps set by the enemy and assures you of a future that is secure and filled with genuine joy and prosperity.

Always remember, God loves everyone deeply. If He didn't care for you, you wouldn't be here, reading this book and seeking a better way to understand His ways. His love is inclusive and far-reaching, extending to every person regardless of their circumstances. Trust in His process and His timing, knowing that His plans are always for your ultimate good and the good of those around you

## ❖ Teaching the word of God for self-defense

Pastors and religious leaders hold a significant responsibility to teach the Word of God in a manner that equips believers for spiritual self-defense. This involves imparting biblical truths that enable individuals to stand firm in their faith, resist temptations, and navigate life's challenges with a godly perspective. Rather than focusing on messages that merely please and comfort, leaders should emphasize teachings that promote spiritual growth and alignment with God's will. It is essential for pastors or any religious leaders to ground their teachings in Scripture. The Bible is the ultimate authority and source of truth until you can prove me wrong. By consistently referring to the Word of God, leaders ensure that their messages are not merely personal opinions but divinely inspired guidance. This approach helps believers develop a solid foundation of biblical knowledge, which is crucial for discernment and spiritual resilience. Religious leaders should emphasize the importance of personal accountability. Teaching believers to take responsibility for their actions and decisions fosters a deeper relationship with God. It encourages introspection and repentance, which are vital for spiritual growth. Pastors should stress that true holiness comes from a heart transformed by God, not from external appearances or mere participation in religious activities. Additionally, leaders must address the reality of sin and its consequences. While it is important to offer messages of hope and encouragement, it is equally important to confront the issues that hinder spiritual progress. By acknowledging sin and its impact, pastors can guide believers toward repentance and the transformative power of God's grace. This balance helps prevent complacency and promotes genuine spiritual maturity. How can we explain that despite having so many believers, the devil still recruits more each day? How can we understand why churches are filled with the devil's agents, who seem unafraid of God's retribution? The best answer lies in the shortcomings of some preaching. The devil exploits these loopholes to recruit and influence church members.

Leaders must critically evaluate the foundation of their churches. ***Was your church built to spread the Word of God and offer spiritual rest to many, or was it established to make money and solve personal financial problems?*** It is crucial to be honest with yourself. You can lie to other people, but you cannot lie God. He knows your thoughts and the true purpose behind building the church. The moment you truly repent, God will be with you, guiding your steps and sending the right people to help cleanse and renew your path. Genuine repentance opens the door to divine intervention, allowing God to purify your intentions and restore your church to its rightful purpose.

When you sincerely turn to God with a repentant heart, He not only forgives but also empowers you to make the necessary changes. His grace will lead you to the right individuals who can assist in casting away any negative influences or corrupt foundations. These divinely appointed helpers will work alongside you, reinforcing your commitment to God's true mission. God's presence will become evident in the renewed focus of your church, shifting from personal gain to genuine spiritual growth and community service. This transformation will attract those who seek true spiritual nourishment and create an environment where God's love and truth can flourish. As you align your church with God's will, the impact on your congregation and community will be profound. Embrace God's guidance and allows Him to reshape your church's foundation ensures that your ministry reflects His glory and purpose. This is a commitment to the authenticity and righteousness that will not only protect your church from the devil's influence but also inspire others to seek God's truth and grace. Trust in God's ability to guide you through this process, knowing that He is always with you, ready to lead and support you on this journey of repentance and renewal.

Now if the primary motivation for establishing a church is financial gain or personal ambition, it leaves a significant opening for the devil to exploit. Such foundations create environments where spiritual integrity is compromised, making it easier for negative influences to take hold. To counter this, churches must recommit to their true purpose: to glorify God and guide people toward genuine spiritual growth. Reevaluate and realign the church's mission with biblical principles is essential. Leaders should focus on preaching the unaltered truth of the Gospel, emphasizing repentance, transformation, and living according to God's commandments. This commitment can help close the loopholes that the devil exploits, creating a more spiritually secure environment for believers. Moreover, pastors or any religious leaders should foster a culture of transparency and accountability within their congregations. Encouraging open dialogue about spiritual challenges and actively addressing issues of sin and temptation can fortify the church against evil influences. When members feel supported and guided in their spiritual journeys, they are less likely to be swayed by the devil's schemes. It is very important for churches to engage in continuous spiritual education, the believers need it. Providing robust discipleship programs and Bible study sessions helps believers deepen their understanding of Scripture and apply its teachings to their lives. Well-informed and spiritually mature members are better equipped to recognize and resist the devil's tactics. A church must focus on building a strong community of faith, where members support and uplift one another. Creating a loving, nurturing environment fosters spiritual resilience and makes it harder for the devil to isolate and influence individuals. Collective prayer, worship, and service activities strengthen the bonds among members and reinforce their commitment to God. Emphasizing the importance of personal spiritual disciplines such as prayer, fasting, and Scripture meditation. Encouraging members to develop these habits strengthens their personal relationship with God and fortifies them against spiritual attacks. When believers are well-grounded in their faith, they are less vulnerable to the devil's recruitment and influence. It is a great idea to address the loopholes in preaching and ensure that the foundation of the church is built on true devotion to God and that are critical steps in protecting believers from the devil's influence. Fostering transparency, continuous education, community support, and personal spiritual disciplines are other steps that churches can take to create an environment where genuine spiritual maturity thrives and the devil's tactics are effectively thwarted. I am not trying to lecture those who might find themselves offended but rather to promote authenticity in leadership, as this is what will build trust and credibility. Teaching the Words of God in a way that equips believers for spiritual self-defense is a profound responsibility. Misleading or confusing them only leads them astray and makes them more vulnerable to the devil, unless leading them away is your agenda from the devil.

This is a prayer to ask God for discernment in choosing where to pray and for taking on responsibilities in a church, if such opportunities exist.

### *Prayer to ask God for clarity and purpose in choosing a place and role within the church*

*Heavenly Father, I come before You seeking Your divine guidance as I consider my place of prayer and the responsibilities I might assume within Your church. Grant me the discernment to recognize the spiritual home where I can grow in faith and contribute most effectively to Your kingdom. Help me understand the needs of the church and where my skills and talents can be best utilized for the greater good.*

*Lord, as I evaluate the opportunities to serve within the church, imbue me with wisdom to make decisions that align with Your will. May the Holy Spirit guide me in this journey, ensuring that my actions and commitments honor You. Give me the foresight to see where I am needed most, and the humility to serve faithfully, recognizing that every role in Your church is vital and valued.*

*Grant me the courage to step up with confidence and the perseverance to fulfill my duties diligently. As I take on responsibilities within Your church, help me to remember that this is not just a duty but a calling to serve You and Your people. May this experience draw me closer to You, deepen my faith, and expand my understanding of what it means to be a part of Your body, the church,*

___ ***In the name of Jesus, I pray,***

____ ***Amen***

Remember, obedience to God is crucial. If you pray and He directs you, embrace His guidance wholeheartedly–there are no insignificant roles in God's kingdom. Even a door greeter may be closer to the gates of heaven than a major contributor. Do not concern yourself with the opinions of others; focus instead on your divine purpose and its significance to God. If you are uncertain about God's response, seek further clarification. Ask Him again the next day, or request that He send His message through someone else, perhaps even in an unexpected encounter on the street or in a casual setting. Rest assured; God is always punctual; a delayed answer does not mean that He is not listening.

## ❖ How to pray effectively and seek God's guidance

I will keep this section brief because there is no single right answer, as God knows us even before we are born. The language you speak, God understands, and He is always listening. He does not sleep and is always on time. Praying effectively and seeking God's guidance is a vital aspect of a strong spiritual life. Prayer is a means of communication with God, a time to express gratitude, seek forgiveness, and ask for His guidance in our lives. Here are several ways to enhance the effectiveness of your prayers and truly seek God's direction. Approach prayer with a heart of humility. Recognize that God is sovereign and all-knowing and approach Him with reverence and respect. Humility allows you to be open to God's will, rather than just seeking to fulfill your own desires. A humble heart is receptive to the guidance and wisdom that God offers.

Consistency in prayer is also crucial. Establish a regular prayer routine, making time each day to connect with God. Whether it's in the morning, during the day, or at night, find a time that works best for you and stick to it. Consistent prayer helps build a deeper relationship with God and keeps your spiritual life grounded. When praying, it is important to be specific. Clearly articulate your thoughts, concerns, and requests to God. Specific prayers allow you to focus on particular areas of your life where you seek guidance or need help. This practice not only makes your prayers more meaningful but also helps you recognize God's answers when they come. Incorporating Scripture into your prayers can enhance their effectiveness. The Bible is filled with promises and examples of God's faithfulness. Praying Scripture, you align your requests with God's Word and His will. This can bring comfort and assurance that God hears you and is working on your behalf.

Listening is a crucial component of effective prayer. Prayer is not just about speaking to God but also about being still and listening for His voice. After you've expressed your thoughts and requests, take time to be silent and attentive to what God might be saying to you. This can come in the form of thoughts, feelings, or even a sense of peace about a decision you need to make. Seeking God's guidance also involves being open to His answers, which may not always align with your expectations. Sometimes, God's response to your prayers might be different from what you anticipated. Be open to His guidance, even if it means taking a path you hadn't considered. Trust that His plans are for your good and His glory. I sometimes encourage community prayer and support as it can also be incredibly beneficial. Praying with others can provide encouragement and additional perspectives. Joining a prayer group or having a prayer partner can help keep you accountable and motivated in your prayer life. The Bible says that where two or three are gathered in His name, He is there among them (Matthew 18:20).

Gratitude is also an essential aspect of prayer. Always take time to thank God for His blessings, both big and small. Gratitude shifts your focus from what you lack to what you have, fostering a positive outlook and strengthening your faith. Thanking God even in challenging times can be a powerful act of faith. You can combine your prayers with fasting as it can also be a powerful tool in seeking God's guidance. Fasting helps you focus spiritually by temporarily giving up something important to you, such as food. This act of sacrifice can heighten your sense of dependence on God and make your prayers more earnest and heartfelt. I do not recommend this, but some people think that keeping a prayer journal can be an effective way to track your prayers and see how God answers them over time. If you prefer this then write down your prayers, reflections, and any insights you receive. This practice can help you stay focused and organized in your prayer life and provide a record of God's faithfulness and guidance.

Repentance is another key aspect of effective prayer. Confess your sins to God and seek His forgiveness. A repentant heart is open and ready to receive God's guidance. Sin can create a barrier between you and God, but confession and repentance restore your relationship with Him. Trust in God's timing, sometimes the answers to our prayers do not come immediately. Trust that God is working in His perfect timing and that He knows what is best for you. Patience and faith are crucial as you wait for His guidance and direction. Remember praying effectively and seeking God's guidance involves humility, consistency, specificity, incorporating Scripture, listening, being open to God's answers, community support, gratitude, fasting, keeping a prayer journal, repentance, and trusting in God's timing.

### *Prayers to seek God's guidance in prayers*

*Heavenly Father, I come before You with a humble heart, seeking Your divine guidance in my prayers. Help me to quiet my mind and open my spirit to Your presence. Grant me the wisdom to know Your will and the strength to follow Your path. Let my words be guided by Your Holy Spirit, and may my prayers align with Your perfect plan for my life. I trust in Your wisdom and timing, Lord.*

*Lord, as I seek Your guidance in prayer, I ask for clarity and understanding. Show me the areas in my life that need Your touch and lead me towards Your truth. Help me to discern Your voice above all others, and give me the courage to act on Your guidance. Thank You for always listening and for being my constant source of strength and comfort.*

**_____ In Jesus' name, I pray.**

**_____ Amen**

# Chapter 6: Practical Steps to Protect Yourself

Protecting yourself against evil influence requires a combination of spiritual practices, personal discipline, and heightened awareness. One of the greatest challenges we all face is fear, and fear is the primary tool the devil uses to disarm and destabilize us. However, if you stand firm in your faith, there is no way that the forces of evil can prevail against you. Remember, those who align with darkness are themselves driven by fear, which is why they operate in secrecy. The Bible reassures us, "Resist the devil, and he will flee from you" (James 4:7). Consider this: if witchcraft were truly powerful, why do practitioners hide their faces? Why do they conceal their actions? Why do they need to call you or friends to see if their plans have succeeded? These questions are difficult to answer because, in the Name of Jesus, witchcraft is powerless. Trust in the Lord and focus on defending yourself with the weapons God has provided and one of these weapons is prayer.

Consistency in prayer is crucial. Being precise and specific in your prayers is even more effective. Broad, generalized prayers lack the potency of specific ones. For example, if you want to pray for financial provision, make it a focused topic. Tell God that this is the issue you are bringing to His table now, acknowledging that there are other concerns, but this is the priority. When praying about finances, you might say:

*"Heavenly Father, I come before You today to seek Your guidance and provision for my financial situation. I trust in Your wisdom and ask for Your help in managing my resources wisely. Please open doors of opportunity and bless me with the means to meet my needs and fulfill my responsibilities. Thank You, Lord, for Your constant provision and care."*

It seems very simple and short, but it is very powerful. This approach not only shows God your specific needs but also demonstrates your trust in His ability to provide. By clearly articulating your concerns, you allow God to work more directly in those areas. Remember, the power of prayer lies in its specificity and consistency. Keep your prayers focused and regular, and trust that God hears and responds to your sincere requests. You do not need hours of prayer; consistency in your prayers is key. You might think, "God already knows my problems, so He will solve them." While it is true that God knows everything about you, it is important to articulate your needs to Him. Just as the devil is aware of your struggles, expressing your concerns in prayer is crucial for witnessing God's intervention. Without voicing your needs, you might be inclined to blame God for not addressing issues you never explicitly brought to Him. Humans can be hypocritical. When they are in need and you help them, it is appreciated. However, when you ask for something in return, they may claim they never asked for your help in the first place–that it was your choice to give. Similarly, in your relationship with God, expressing your needs through prayer acknowledges your dependence on Him and opens the door for His blessings and guidance.

Prayer is not about informing God of what He already knows; it is about building a relationship with Him, showing your faith, and acknowledging your reliance on His wisdom and power. Consistent, specific prayers demonstrate your trust in God's ability to provide and your willingness to engage in a meaningful dialogue with Him. By doing so, you create a space for God to manifest His will in your life, addressing your needs and guiding you on your spiritual journey.

Understand that nothing in life is free; you must work diligently to earn everything. Even when you ask God for blessings, He expects you to put in effort and dedication. Prayer is the first step, but action must follow. By aligning your hard work with God's guidance, you open yourself up to the blessings He has in store for you.

When you ask God for His help, remember that He also desires something from you in return. What God seeks is not material wealth or grand gestures, but rather recognition and obedience. Acknowledge His sovereignty in your life and strive to live according to His commandments.

This obedience reflects your faith and trust in His wisdom, demonstrating your commitment to His will. In recognizing God's role in your life, you cultivate a heart of gratitude and humility. This recognition is a form of worship, honoring God for His continuous presence and support. It is through this reverence that you build a deeper relationship with Him, one that goes beyond mere requests and enters the realm of true communion. Your obedience is a testament to your faith, showing that you not only seek God's gifts but also His guidance and direction. The cycle of asking and receiving from God is strengthened by your willingness to give back through recognition and obedience. By doing so, you align yourself more closely with His divine plan, ensuring that your efforts are blessed, and your path is illuminated by His grace. This mutual exchange fosters a dynamic and fulfilling relationship with God, where both your earthly endeavors and spiritual aspirations are nurtured and supported.

One point I want to emphasize is the mistake many people make when they rely on someone else to pray for them. Before anyone prays on your behalf, you must grant them the permission to speak to God for you, and you implicitly agree with whatever they say, whether they accurately represent your situation or not. This can be risky, as they might misrepresent your needs or intentions. Take your relationship with God seriously. If others can talk to God, so can you. He is our Father, the King of Kings, the Supreme Ruler of the universe. He loves you deeply and will hear your prayers, no matter your past sins. Approach Him directly with faith, honesty, and repentance, and He will listen. Remember, God desires a personal relationship with each of His children. While it is beneficial to have others pray for you, it should never replace your own communication with God. Your direct prayers are a way to build and strengthen your personal relationship with Him, ensuring that your true heart's intentions are conveyed. Be faithful, honest, and repentant in your prayers. God is always ready to listen and respond to a sincere heart. By taking responsibility for your spiritual journey and speaking directly to

God, you demonstrate your trust in His love and power. This personal connection with God is invaluable and irreplaceable, fostering a deeper and more authentic faith.

Please stop relying solely on your pastor; he is not God. He is a servant, a minister of the Gospel, a mandated one, but he is not divine. He is far from perfect. Like you, he navigates the challenges of daily life and sometimes, your voice might be heard more clearly by God, especially if your pastor is not aligned with God's will. Many people love prophecy and seek to hear only positive things from their pastor's mouth, but often, these pastors might avoid telling you the hard truths about your behavior and why you feel distant from God. Unfortunately, some pastors are merely agents of the devil, and this is not a new revelation. The Bible warns that false prophets will come disguised as servants of righteousness, making it difficult to recognize them. Be aware of these individuals. These deceptive pastors might use evil means to infiltrate your life, but remember, they need your permission to gain access. Once they are in, they build connections that allow the devil to manipulate you.

It is crucial to understand that your direct relationship with God is paramount. While pastors can provide guidance and support, they should not be your sole connection to God. You have the same ability to pray, seek, and receive guidance from God as anyone else. Do not give others undue power over your spiritual life. Be vigilant and discerning about who you allow to influence your spiritual journey. Align yourself with the true teachings of the Bible and cultivate a personal relationship with God through prayer, study, and obedience. This personal connection will protect you from deception and help you grow in faith and righteousness.

Have you noticed that every time someone wants to prophesy over you, they always ask, "Can I do it? Can I speak?" This is because they cannot break the spiritual law by entering your life without your permission. You hold the power to accept or reject their influence. If you feel that a prophecy is not meant for you, do not accept it.

The moment you say yes, you are essentially agreeing that what they say is true, and it can manifest in your life because the Bible says,

*"Truly I tell you, whatever you bind on earth will be bound in heaven, and whatever you loose on earth will be loosed in heaven." **Matthew 18:18***

Be careful about whom you allow into your spiritual life. If a prophecy does not resonate with you or feels incorrect, do not be afraid to reject it. The authority over your life is given by the Almighty, and no one has power over you except Him. Stand firm in your faith and trust in your own relationship with God. It is essential to be discerning and protective of your spiritual space. The Bible teaches us to test every spirit and to be cautious of false prophets. Do not be intimidated or pressured into accepting a prophecy that does not align with your understanding or feels wrong. Your spiritual well-being is paramount, and God has given you the wisdom to discern His truth. Remember, your life is governed by God's divine plan. Trust in His guidance and seek His counsel directly. You have the right and the responsibility to safeguard your spiritual journey, ensuring that it remains true to God's purpose for you.

Lastly, do not allow pastors or others to lay their hands on your head while praying for you. This practice is not recommended, as it can open you up to potential harm. Some may use this act to initiate you into something without your knowledge, take your grace or blessings, or transfer negativity into your life. The effects may not be immediate; you might notice a gradual decline in your life, moving downward, without realizing that you granted access to your innermost being. *Use your own hand and put on your heart. You are not required to close your eyes, closing eyes is to avoid distraction.* Your head is precious, holding both your thoughts and your spiritual essence. Allowing someone to touch your head can potentially dim your spiritual light. You may not fully understand how prepared these agents of the devil are. Infiltrating churches and communities, they seek to get close to people and expand their influence. Your loss becomes their gain, and if they succeed in leading you away from the light, they are rewarded for their efforts. Protect yourself and maintain a discerning spirit. Understand that the devil's agents are cunning and may appear as righteous individuals. Be vigilant and cautious, safeguarding your spiritual well-being against those who might wish to harm you. If you wonder why they don't have to touch your head, well, here are some reasons:

The head holds significant spiritual meaning in many religious and cultural traditions.

## 1. Seat of Thought and Consciousness

The head is often considered the center of thought, intellect, and consciousness. It represents the mind and the ability to think, reason, and make decisions. In spiritual terms, it is the place where divine inspiration and wisdom can be received.

## 2. Symbol of Authority and Leadership

In many traditions, the head symbolizes authority and leadership. Kings and leaders are often anointed on the head, signifying their divine right to rule and their connection to higher powers. The head is seen as the focal point of one's identity and power.

### 3. Connection to the Divine

The head is often viewed as the part of the body closest to the divine. In many spiritual practices, the top of the head (the crown chakra in Hinduism and Buddhism) is believed to be the point where individuals connect with higher consciousness and spiritual enlightenment.

### 4. Protection and Blessings

The act of placing hands on someone's head during a blessing or prayer is seen as a way to confer spiritual protection, guidance, and blessings. However, it can also be a point of vulnerability if the person laying hands on the head has negative intentions.

### 5. Symbol of Spiritual Armor

In Christian teachings, the "helmet of salvation" (Ephesians 6:17) is part of the full armor of God. This symbolizes the protection of one's mind and thoughts through faith and salvation, guarding against spiritual attacks and deception.

### 6. Source of Vision and Perception

The head houses the eyes, ears, nose, and mouth, which are the primary senses through which we perceive the world. Spiritually, this means the head is associated with insight, discernment, and the ability to receive and process spiritual truths and revelations.

### 7. Center of Personal Identity

The head, and more specifically the face, is often seen as the representation of an individual's identity and soul. It is where one's personality, expressions, and emotions are most visibly displayed, making it a crucial aspect of one's spiritual and personal existence.

Again, trust in God's protection and seek His guidance directly. Your relationship with Him is personal and sacred. Stay connected to God and be aware of the potential risks, you can avoid falling prey to those who seek to exploit your faith for their own gain. In case you cannot avoid it or it might surprise you do this prayer up front before going in that church or event.

### Prayer for Protection Against Devil Agents

*Heavenly Father, I come before You today seeking Your divine protection against any agents of the devil who may seek to harm or deceive me. Cover me with Your holy presence and shield me with Your mighty power. Let Your angels encamp around me, guarding me from all evil. Grant me the wisdom and discernment to recognize any malicious intentions and the strength to stand firm in Your truth*

**_____ In the Name of Jesus**

**___ Amen.**

### Prayer for Discernment Against False Pastors and Prophecies

*Lord Jesus, You are the Good Shepherd, and I trust in Your guidance and protection. As I prepare to attend church or a prayer event, I ask for Your discernment to identify any false pastors or misleading prophecies. Fill me with the Holy Spirit, so that I may see clearly and not be swayed by those who do not speak Your truth. Help me to listen to Your voice above all others and follow the path You have set for me.*

_**In the Name of Jesus**_

_**Amen.**_

### _Prayer for Safeguarding Against the Devil's Plans_

_Almighty God, I know that the enemy has plans to deceive and destroy, but I trust in Your greater plan for my life. Before I step into any spiritual gathering, I ask for Your protection against the devil's schemes. Surround me with Your light and truth, and let no weapon formed against me prosper. Strengthen my faith and fill my heart with Your peace, knowing that You are my refuge and fortress._

_**In Jesus' name, I pray.**_

_**Amen.**_

# Part 3

## Reclaiming Your Life

# Chapter 7: Breaking Curses and Reclaiming Prosperity

Curses, both spoken and unspoken, can have a profound impact on our lives, often leading to a cycle of misfortune and hardship. These curses can stem from generational issues, negative words spoken over us, or even our own actions and beliefs. Recognizing and breaking these curses is essential for reclaiming the prosperity and abundance that God intends for each of us. This chapter will guide you through understanding the nature of curses, how they affect our lives, and the steps you can take to break free from their hold. The concept of curses may seem archaic to some of you, but their effects are very real and present in our lives today. A curse is essentially a negative spiritual force that can hinder our progress, bring about misfortune, and block the blessings that God has in store for us. These curses can manifest in various ways, such as financial struggles, health issues, broken relationships, and a general sense of stagnation. I will discuss little more breaking curse as it involves a combination of spiritual practices, personal reflection, and practical steps. It begins with identifying the curse and its origin. This might involve looking into your family history, examining your own life for patterns of negativity, and seeking divine revelation through prayer. Once the curse is identified, you can begin the process of breaking it through repentance, forgiveness, and renouncing any agreements or beliefs that have allowed the curse to take hold.

Prayer is a powerful tool in breaking curses. Through fervent and specific prayers, you can call upon God's power to break the chains of curses and release His blessings into your life. Scriptures such as Galatians 3:13 remind us that Christ has redeemed us from the curse of the law by becoming a curse for us. Standing on these promises, you can declare freedom from curses and reclaim the prosperity that God has promised. Start making positive declarations and affirmations over your life. Speak words of life, abundance, and blessing, aligning your words with God's promises. Reject any negative words or beliefs that have been spoken over you, and replace them with affirmations of God's love, provision, and purpose for your life. This practice helps to rewire your mindset and align your life with God's truth. Breaking curses and reclaiming prosperity involve taking practical steps to change your circumstances. I will try to explain a little more with prayers to claim your prosperity. This might include seeking financial advice, improving your health, repairing relationships, and making wise decisions in your daily life. By combining spiritual practices with practical actions, you can create an environment where prosperity can flourish. Remember, God's desire is for you to live a life of abundance and blessing, free from the bondage of curses. With faith, determination, and the right steps, you can break free and reclaim the prosperity that is rightfully yours.

## ❖ How to recognize and rebuke curses?

Recognizing a curse is the first step toward breaking free from its grip and reclaiming the prosperity God intends for you. Curses can manifest in various aspects of your life, such as persistent financial troubles, chronic health issues, relational conflicts, and continuous failures or setbacks despite your best efforts. These patterns are often indicative of a deeper spiritual problem that needs to be addressed. One of the keyways to recognize a curse is through repeated misfortunes or failures that seem inexplicable. As an example, if you notice that despite your hard work and dedication, you continually face financial ruin or loss, this could be a sign of a financial curse. Similarly, if you and your family members suffer from recurring illnesses that defy medical explanation, there might be a generational curse at play. These patterns, when persistent and unexplained by natural causes, warrant a deeper spiritual investigation.

Another indicator of a curse is an unexplainable heaviness or feeling of oppression. This can manifest as a constant state of anxiety, depression, or a sense of being trapped in a negative cycle. It might feel like a cloud of negativity that follows you, regardless of positive changes or efforts. This spiritual oppression can drain your energy and hope, making it difficult to see a way out. Recognizing this feeling is crucial, as it often points to a spiritual root that needs to be addressed. Once you have identified the possible presence of a curse, the next step is to seek God's guidance through prayer. Ask God to reveal the source of the curse and to provide wisdom and discernment. Prayer is a powerful tool that invites God's intervention and opens the door for divine revelation. Spend time in quiet reflection and listen for God's direction. He may reveal specific incidents, generational patterns, or personal sins that need to be addressed.

Repentance is another critical component in breaking a curse. Acknowledge any sins or wrongful actions that may have opened the door to the curse. This could involve personal sins, involvement in occult practices, or unforgiveness. Confess these sins to God and seek His forgiveness. The Bible assures us in 1 John 1:9 that if we confess our sins, He is faithful and just to forgive us and cleanse us from all unrighteousness. This act of repentance breaks the legal hold that the curse has on your life. After repentance, it is time to renounce any agreements or covenants made, knowingly or unknowingly, that have allowed the curse to take hold. This involves verbally rejecting and breaking any ties to sinful behaviors, occult practices, or generational curses. *Speak out loud, declaring your rejection of these influences and affirming your allegiance to God alone*. This verbal declaration is a powerful act of spiritual warfare that severs the ties binding you to the curse. Let me explain clearly this part as it could help in many ways.

### The Power of Verbal Declaration in Breaking Curses

When you speak out loud to declare your rejection of negative influences and affirm your allegiance to God alone, you engage in a powerful act of spiritual warfare. This verbal declaration is not just a formality but a significant spiritual action that has profound implications. Here's a clearer explanation of why this practice is so powerful and how it works:

- **■ Taking Authority in the Spiritual Realm:** Speaking out loud is a way to assert your authority in the spiritual realm. According to the Bible, our words have power. Proverbs 18:21 states, "The tongue has the power of life and death." By verbally rejecting curses and negative influences, you are using the power of your words to break their hold over you. This act signifies that you are taking control and refusing to allow these negative forces to dictate your life

- **■ Severing Ties to Negative Influences:** Curses and negative influences often form spiritual ties that bind individuals to their effects. When you verbally declare your rejection of these influences, you are actively cutting these ties. This declaration serves as a spiritual severance, breaking the connection that the curse or negative influence has over your life. It is akin to saying, *"I no longer* *accept this bondage, and I sever all connections to it.*"

- **Affirming Allegiance to God:** In the same declaration, affirming your allegiance to God alone is crucial. This affirmation not only rejects the negative influence but also reaffirms your commitment to God's authority and protection. James 4:7 advises, "*Submit yourselves, then, to God. Resist the devil, and he will flee from you.*" By declaring your allegiance to God, you align yourself with His power and protection, effectively resisting the devil and his schemes

- **Engaging in Spiritual Warfare:** Spiritual warfare involves battling against forces of darkness that seek to harm or hinder us. Verbal declarations are a key tactic in this battle. Ephesians 6:17 refers to the "sword of the Spirit, which is the word of God." When you speak God's truths and reject lies and curses, you are wielding this spiritual sword. This proactive stance weakens the enemy's grip and empowers you to stand firm in your faith.

■ **Reinforcing Your Faith and Resolve:** Speaking out loud also reinforces your own faith and resolve. Hearing yourself declare rejection of curses and affirmation of God's power strengthens your belief in these truths. It helps to internalize your commitment and boosts your confidence in God's ability to protect and bless you. This reinforcement is essential in maintaining the freedom you gain from breaking curses.

■ **Creating a Spiritual Shift:** Verbal declarations create a shift in the spiritual atmosphere. When you speak words of truth and power, you invite God's presence and align yourself with His will. This shift can bring about significant changes in your circumstances, opening the door for blessings and breakthroughs that were previously hindered by curses or negative influences

### *How to Make a Verbal Declaration?*

To make a verbal declaration, find a quiet and private place where you can speak freely. Begin by praying for God's presence and guidance. Then, clearly and firmly state your rejection of the specific curses or negative influences you have identified. For example, you might say:

*"In the name of Jesus, I reject and renounce any curses or negative influences over my life. I break all ties and connections to these forces. I affirm my allegiance to God alone, and I declare that I am free from all bondage through His power and grace. I welcome God's blessings, protection, and guidance in my life.*

*\_\_\_\_ Amen."*

Remember to replace the curse with God's blessings through prayer and positive declarations. *Speak blessings over your life, health, finances, and relationships, aligning your words with God's promises in the Bible.* Scriptures like Deuteronomy 28:13, which states that the Lord will make you the head and not the tail, are powerful affirmations of God's intended blessings. By consistently speaking life and blessings, you reinforce your spiritual breakthrough and invite God's favor. Don't forget to ask assistance to others members, and this why it is good to surround yourself with a supportive faith community. Breaking a curse can be a challenging journey, and having the support of fellow believers can provide encouragement and accountability. Engage in regular worship, prayer groups, and Bible studies. Share your journey with trusted spiritual mentors who can pray with you and offer guidance. The power of collective prayer and support cannot be underestimated in maintaining your newfound freedom and continuing to walk in God's blessings.

## ❖ Steps to reclaim your prosperity, family, and finances

Reclaiming your prosperity, family, and finances requires a holistic approach that combines spiritual, emotional, and practical steps. It begins with a firm belief that God desires abundance and well-being for you in every area of your life. When you align yourself with His promises and taking actionable steps, you can begin to see positive changes and restoration. Here are some steps, not all of them but, these steps can be helpful. Reclaiming your prosperity, family, and finances requires a holistic approach that combines spiritual, emotional, and practical steps. It begins with a firm belief that God desires abundance and well-being for you in every area of your life. The first step in reclaiming your prosperity is to strengthen your faith and trust in God. Recognize that God is your ultimate provider and that He has plans to prosper you and not to harm you (Jeremiah 29:11). Spend time in prayer and meditation, seeking His guidance and asking for the wisdom to manage your resources effectively.

Identify any negative cycles or curses that may be affecting your prosperity, family, and finances. This could be generational patterns of poverty, broken relationships, or poor financial decisions. Through prayer and repentance, break these negative cycles and renounce any curses. Declare God's promises over your life, family, and finances, and believe that He can bring restoration and renewal. Create a budget, diligently track your expenses, and prioritize your spending. If possible, allocate funds to pay your tithe, ensuring that this commitment does not impact your essential monthly living expenses. Managing your money wisely allows you to fulfill your spiritual obligations while maintaining financial stability. Seek financial advice if needed and make informed decisions about saving, investing, and reducing debt. Managing your finances wisely, you create a stable foundation that supports your overall well-being and enables you to provide for your family. Strengthening family relationships is essential for reclaiming your prosperity. Invest time and effort in nurturing your relationships with family members. Communicate openly, show love and respect, and work together to overcome challenges. It is also important to cultivate a mindset of abundance rather than scarcity. Believe that God wants to bless you abundantly and that there is enough for everyone. This positive mindset can transform the way you approach challenges and opportunities, enabling you to see possibilities rather than limitations. Here a prayer to help you overcome this situation.

## Powerful Prayer for Reclaiming Prosperity, Family, and Finances

**Heavenly Father**, I come before You with a heart full of faith, seeking Your divine intervention in my life. I declare Your promises over my prosperity, family, and finances. In the name of Jesus, I break every curse and negative cycle that has hindered my progress. I renounce any agreements with poverty, strife, and lack, and I embrace Your abundant blessings.

Lord, grant me the wisdom to manage my finances wisely and the strength to overcome any obstacles. Restore and heal my family relationships, bringing unity, love, and understanding into our home. Open the windows of heaven and pour out Your blessings upon me, so that I may live in the fullness of Your provision.

I trust in Your plan for my life, knowing that You are my provider and protector. Thank You, Lord, for Your faithfulness and for the miracles that You are working in my life right now. I receive Your blessings with gratitude and joy.

*In Jesus' name, I pray*

*Amen.*

## ❖ Practical advice for maintaining spiritual health

Maintaining spiritual health is essential for overall well-being and resilience in the face of life's challenges. Here are some practical steps to help you nurture and sustain your spiritual vitality:

### 1. Daily Prayer and Meditation

One of the most effective ways to maintain spiritual health is through daily prayer and meditation. Prayer is a direct line of communication with God, allowing you to express gratitude, seek guidance, and find comfort. Meditation helps you to quiet your mind and focus on God's presence. Setting aside specific times each day for these practices can significantly enhance your spiritual connection and provide peace and clarity amidst the chaos of everyday life. It doesn't have to be a long prayer or meditation. Remember, the quality of your prayers matters more than their length. You can pray even while walking, for God is omnipresent–available at any time, always punctual in His responses. Simply call out to Him, and He will be there for you. You hold a special place in God's heart, and He cherishes every moment you reach out to Him.

## 2. Regular Scripture Reading

Engaging with the Bible regularly is crucial for spiritual growth. The Scriptures offer wisdom, encouragement, and instructions for living a life that honors God. Whether it's reading a passage in the morning to start your day or studying a chapter in-depth in the evening, regular Scripture reading helps to ground you in God's truth. Additionally, memorizing verses can be a powerful tool for spiritual fortification, providing strength and guidance in times of need. Don't worry, it might take some time but it is never late to start.

## 3. Active Participation in a Faith Community

Being part of a faith community provides support, accountability, and fellowship. Regularly attending worship services, Bible studies, and prayer groups helps you to stay connected with other believers who can encourage and challenge you in your faith journey. Sharing experiences and learning from others fosters a sense of belonging and helps you to grow spiritually. It also provides opportunities to serve and support others, which can be spiritually enriching.

## 4. Practice Gratitude and Positivity

Cultivating a heart of gratitude and maintaining a positive outlook are vital for spiritual health. Regularly acknowledging and thanking God for His blessings, both big and small, shifts your focus from what you lack to what you have. This practice can transform your perspective, reduce stress, and increase your sense of joy and contentment. Positivity helps you to see God's hand in every situation, fostering a deeper trust and reliance on Him. We are always focused on what we don't have rather than appreciating what God provided already. We are not grateful for what we have and we don't even used to the fullest and we kept asking more and more every day. Take time to value what you have and look back on what you had before. You will see what God has done for you and your family. Greed can lead you astray. Do not think that you are a failure because you are not successful after many years. Instead, ask yourself, have I invited God to control things? Sometimes, you think you have control until you realize that you got it all wrong.

## 5. Healthy Lifestyle Choices

Your physical health can significantly impact your spiritual well-being. Engaging in regular physical activity, eating a balanced diet, and getting adequate rest are essential for maintaining the energy and mental clarity needed for spiritual practices. Avoiding substances and behaviors that can harm your body helps to keep you physically and spiritually fit. A healthy lifestyle supports a clear mind and a receptive spirit, making it easier to connect with God and sustain your spiritual health.

### 6. Continuous Learning and Growth

Commit to continuous learning and growth in your spiritual life. Attend seminars, read books, and listen to podcasts that deepen your understanding of the faith. Seek mentorship from mature believers who can offer guidance and insight. Embrace opportunities for spiritual retreats and personal reflection. By continually seeking to learn and grow, you keep your faith vibrant and dynamic, always moving closer to God and deeper in your spiritual journey.

# Chapter 8: Closing the Door to the Devil

Closing the door to the devil is essential for maintaining spiritual health and protecting oneself from negative influences. This process involves a combination of spiritual vigilance, personal discipline, and the active cultivation of a relationship with God. Once you understand the devil's tactics and reinforcing your spiritual defenses, you can effectively close the door to his influence. In Chapter One, I discussed how the devil's agents operate. To summarize, it is crucial to understand that the devil often employs subtle tactics and lies to gain a foothold in your life. This can include temptation, deceit, and manipulation of circumstances to lead you away from God's path. Being aware of these tactics is essential before you can effectively think about closing the door to the devil. Indeed, while it might seem straightforward to close one door, the risk of inadvertently opening another to the devil is high if you do not fully grasp how he operates. The devil is adept at exploiting our vulnerabilities, finding new ways to infiltrate our lives when we least expect it. It is important to recognize that the devil himself can open doors due to our inherent weaknesses and vulnerabilities.

Indeed, while it might seem straightforward to close one door, the risk of inadvertently opening another to the devil is high if you do not fully grasp how he operates. The devil is adept at exploiting our vulnerabilities, finding new ways to infiltrate our lives when we least expect it. It is important to recognize that the devil himself can open doors due to our inherent weaknesses and vulnerabilities. The devil's primary goal is to separate us from God, and he will use any means necessary to achieve this. It is important to recognize and understand his methods as we can better guard ourselves against his influence. This includes being aware of how he uses lies and manipulation to create doubt, fear, and confusion in our minds

## ❖ Identifying ways we Unknowingly Invite the Devil into Our Lives

Often, without realizing it, we can inadvertently open the door to the devil in our lives through our actions, thoughts, and habits. Recognizing these gateways is crucial in fortifying our spiritual defenses and maintaining a strong relationship with God. One of the most common ways we invite the devil in is through harboring negative emotions such as anger, bitterness, and unforgiveness. These feelings can fester and grow, creating a foothold for the devil to exploit. The Bible warns us about the dangers of allowing anger to linger, stating in Ephesians 4:26-27, "Do not let the sun go down while you are still angry, and do not give the devil a foothold.

You might be surprised about how the media and entertainment influence our lives. Yes, we often unknowingly invite the devil into our lives through our consumption of media and entertainment. The content we watch, read, and listen can significantly impact our thoughts and behaviors. Engaging with media that glorifies violence, immorality, or occult practices can desensitize us to sin and open us up to negative spiritual influences. It is essential to be discerning about the media we consume and ensure it aligns with our values and faith. Engaging in occult practices or dabbling in seemingly harmless activities such as horoscopes, tarot cards, or spirit communication can also invite the devil into our lives. These practices open doors to spiritual realms that are not of God and can lead to dangerous spiritual consequences. The Bible explicitly warns against such practices in Deuteronomy 18:10-12, where it condemns divination, sorcery, and seeking omens. These practices affect the way you approach problems and challenges in life. When faced with even a minor issue, whether self-created or a test from the Lord, you might panic and seek refuge in tarot card readings or other forms of divination instead of turning to God. This reliance on the occult diverts you from the faith and trust you should place in God.

Media consumption is another subtle way we invite negative influences into our lives. Watching television, browsing social media, and listening to music often means consenting to be exposed to various content, some of which may be harmful to our spiritual well-being. These media forms can present materials and images that desensitize us to sin and lead us away from God's teachings. Some content is intentionally designed to lead you down an infinite journey of distraction and spiritual erosion, all without you being fully aware of its impact. When you watch TV, you open yourself up to a vast array of content that can shape your thoughts and behaviors, often in ways contrary to your faith. Similarly, social media can bombard you with images and messages that promote envy, materialism, and other negative emotions. The music you listen to can also carry messages that influence your mood and mindset, steering you away from a focus on God. These influences can subtly shift your values and priorities, making it easier for the devil to gain a foothold in your life. How many times have you found yourself endlessly scrolling through infinite reels on social media, each one more captivating than the last? The more you scroll, the deeper your interest becomes, drawing you further into a cycle of distraction. This seemingly innocuous habit can consume hours of your day, diverting your attention from meaningful activities and spiritual growth. By continually exposing yourself to media that contradicts God's Word, you become more susceptible to spiritual attacks.

Engaging also with media that glorifies sin can weaken your spiritual defenses. Movies, shows, and music that celebrate immoral behavior can desensitize you to sin and make it seem more acceptable. Over time, this can erode your moral compass and lead you away from God's path. Be mindful of the media you engage with and choose content that uplifts and strengthens your faith. I am not saying that everything from the media is evil or to watch tv or avoid social media. What I am emphasizing is the use of anything we have. You must know what we want and not just consume everything on your plate. You just have to recognize that media consumption is not just passive; it involves active participation. By watching, browsing, and listening, you are engaging with the content and allowing it to influence you. Take control of your media habits and ensure that what you consume supports your spiritual growth and aligns with God's teachings. We can invite the devil into our lives through complacency and neglect our spiritual disciplines. When we become lax in our prayer life, Bible study, and fellowship with other believers, we weaken our spiritual defenses. This spiritual neglect creates vulnerabilities that the devil can exploit. Staying consistent and diligent in your spiritual practices is the key to maintain a strong and vibrant relationship with God.

## ❖ Close the doors permanently to unhealthy relationships and influences

Unhealthy relationships and influences can serve as entry points for the devil. Associating closely with individuals who lead us away from

God's principles can negatively impact our spiritual walk. These relationships can introduce doubt, temptation, and sinful behaviors into our lives. Some people may tend to convince you that God does not exist, and the Bible is just a book like any other book. They will engage a debate that may confused you, they will talk more and give you less time to talk or explain. We will try to upset you because you do not accept what they are saying and trying to convince them. My advice is that if you are convinced of God's existence, avoid engaging in debates with those who have a different agenda. These individuals are often seeking followers to validate their beliefs, even when they know those beliefs are false. Consider how they managed to convince some that same-sex marriage should be accepted in the church while polygamy and polyandry are not. It often starts with the argument of individual rights, but there is usually much more hidden behind the scenes. Some people might be pressured into endorsing certain beliefs due to compromising or damaging evidence that could end their careers or disrupt their families. This coercion can lead to the acceptance of practices that are contrary to traditional religious teachings. Therefore, it's crucial to stand firm in your faith and be discerning about the discussions and debates you engage in. When confronted with these situations, remember that your faith and beliefs should be rooted in the teachings of the Bible and the guidance of the Holy Spirit, not the shifting opinions of society. Be wary of those who seek to undermine your convictions for their own gain. Engaging in debates with those who have ulterior motives can be draining and unproductive. Instead, focus your energy on strengthening your relationship with God and sharing your faith through actions and genuine conversations with those open to learning. Avoid debates that aim to distort your beliefs and lure you into false validations. Stay true to your faith, be discerning, and focus on nurturing your relationship with God.

**Example 1: Toxic Friendships**

One example of an unhealthy relationship that can undermine someone's faith is a toxic friendship. Imagine having a close friend who consistently belittles your beliefs, mocks your values, and encourages behaviors that go against your faith. This friend might invite you to activities that involve excessive drinking, promiscuity, or other actions that compromise your moral standards. Over time, the influence of this friend can lead you to question your convictions, participate in harmful behaviors, and drift away from your spiritual practices. The constant exposure to negativity and discouragement can erode your confidence in your faith and weaken your relationship with God.

**Example 2: Romantic Relationships with Non-Believers**

Another example is a romantic relationship with a non-believer who is openly hostile to your faith. Suppose you are dating someone who not only does not share your religious beliefs but also actively discourages you from practicing your faith. This partner may criticize your participation in church activities, ridicule your prayer habits, or try to persuade you to adopt their secular worldview. They can even threaten you to break up if you kept talking about an invisible God and Jesus. They might pressure you to skip church services, engage in behaviors that conflict with your values, or abandon your spiritual commitments altogether. Such a relationship can create significant spiritual conflict, pulling you away from your faith community and leading to spiritual isolation and confusion. Do not fall for it; it is a trap. If you live with someone and notice they are always upset when you pray, it is a clear sign that they may be on the opposing side spiritually. Physically, you might be friends, boyfriend and girlfriend, or even husband and wife, but in reality, you are enemies in the spiritual realm because you are not aligned with their beliefs. This disparity creates an environment of constant tension and discord, which can erode your spiritual well-being over time. You may find yourself compromising your values to keep the peace or avoid conflict, gradually drifting away from your faith and the practices that nurture your relationship with God. The spiritual warfare in such relationships is subtle yet powerful, aiming to weaken your resolve and separate you from your divine purpose.

Here a powerful prayer to help you with toxic relationship.

### *Prayer for Guidance and Strength in a Toxic Relationship*

**Heavenly Father**, *I come before You with a heavy heart, burdened by the challenges in my romantic relationship. Lord, You know my struggles and the pain I feel. I ask for Your divine wisdom and discernment to see clearly the path You want me to take. Help me to understand Your will and to have the strength to follow it, even when it is difficult. Surround me with Your peace, which surpasses all understanding, and guide my steps towards healing and restoration.*

*Lord Jesus, You are my rock and my refuge. In this time of turmoil, I seek Your protection from the toxic influences that threaten my emotional and spiritual well-being. Grant me the courage to set healthy boundaries and to stand firm in my faith, despite the pressures I face. Help me to remember that I am fearfully and wonderfully made, and that my worth is found in You alone. Fill me with Your love and grace, so that I can extend forgiveness where needed, but also have the wisdom to make decisions that honor You.*

*Holy Spirit, empower me with Your strength and guidance. Illuminate the areas of my life that need Your healing touch, and help me to let go of any unhealthy attachments. Give me the courage to trust in Your plan for my future, knowing that You desire only the best for me. Lead me to relationships that are edifying and rooted in Your truth. I pray for the salvation of my partner, that they may come to know You and experience the transformative power of Your love.*

**__ In Jesus' name, I pray,**

**__ Amen.**

## ❖ How to help others recognize and defend themselves against spiritual attacks

Spiritual attacks are often subtle and can manifest in various ways, such as feelings of intense fear, doubt, confusion, and temptation. When someone is under the influence of the devil, they may be completely unaware of it, sometimes not realizing it until it's too late or until God intervenes to pull them out of the darkness. These attacks are exceptionally subtle, ensnaring individuals in a complex labyrinth of deception and despair from which escape seems almost impossible. Many people suffer silently in these situations, unable to trust anyone enough to seek help. These victims often turn their frustration and anger towards God, blaming Him for their broken lives, while failing to acknowledge their own role in opening the door to the devil's influence. This rejection of personal responsibility further entraps them, making it even harder to find their way back to divine protection and peace.

To help someone under a spiritual attack, it is essential to ask for their consent before any prayer or intervention. The reason for this is that they might be fully aware of their situation and could be in a spiritual pact that, if broken without their agreement, could have severe consequences. In some cases, the person may have been cursed due to wrongdoing or out of someone else's jealousy. Once they agree, you can begin praying for them in the name of Jesus, explicitly stating that you have their consent and that they are rejecting this current state of bondage. *I will provide a prayer below to assist you, but please proceed with caution, as you can become a target of the spirit afflicting them*. When you start praying for someone, you may not know the depth of their bond or the source of their spiritual issues. The spirit controlling them may attack you, and the only safeguard against this is the clear, verbal consent of the individual, such as, "I am doing this because he/she has given me their consent to pray for them." This declaration is crucial as it establishes your authority to intervene on their behalf. Many men of God have lost their lives in these situations, and others trying to help have been physically attacked, losing their vision, becoming paralyzed, and suffering other severe consequences. It is often recommended not to attempt deliverance alone; it is better to work as a team. You may not know the type of spirit involved in the bondage, and it can be risky. However, if God sends you specifically for the deliverance, then you have been mandated to go. Do not be afraid; the Lord has your back. In such cases, anything you say is justified, and you do not even need the person's consent because the Lord has sent you. However, be cautious if someone claims, "The Lord told me." I recommend that you seek the Lord's guidance personally; do not just follow them blindly. Generally, God will provide you with a sign or you will receive the same message about the mission. Beware of pastors using the devil to deliver people in these situations; they are numerous. They may appear to solve a problem but often create another. The victim might recover, but at what price? You could receive your deliverance only to lose your leg in an accident a month later. This is not a coincidence; it is their law. However, when God delivers you, there is no sacrifice. You are forever free unless you open the door again. Here is a prayer you can use:

### *Prayer for Deliverance*

***Heavenly Father**, I come before You in the mighty name of Jesus Christ. I thank You for Your love and mercy. Today, I lift up [Name] to You, who has given me their consent to pray on their behalf. Lord, I ask for Your divine protection over both of us as we proceed.*

*Lord Jesus, by the power of Your blood and Your sacrifice on the cross, we reject and renounce any spirit or curse that has bound [Name]. We declare that they are free from any pacts, curses, or spiritual bonds that have kept them captive. In Jesus' name, we command any evil spirit to leave [Name] and never return.*

*Holy Spirit, fill [state the Name] with Your peace, love, and protection. Surround us with Your angels and shield us from any counterattacks. We place our trust in You, knowing that You are our protector and deliverer. Thank You, Lord, for Your faithfulness and power.*

___ **In Jesus' name, I pray.**

___ **Amen**

Very important: make sure you do some follow up to accompany him taking the road and new path of light. Teach him how to pray and what prayer to use in every situation. There is another book, eBook and App (available on both Play store and App Store) with the prayers available. You can request prayers.

Book title: ***"The Perfect Prayers: A Path to Spiritual Fulfillment"***

# Chapter 9: Living Life to the Fullest

Living life to the fullest involves embracing each moment with purpose, joy, and intentionality. It means making the most of your time, relationships, and opportunities while staying true to your values and beliefs. A positive mindset is foundational to living a fulfilling life. Focus on the good in every situation and practice gratitude daily. Positive thinking not only improves your mental health but also attracts more positivity into your life. Often, we spend our time focusing on unnecessary worries and denying ourselves the joys and blessings God wants us to experience. God desires for you to live a wonderful life full of grace and good things that empower you and positively impact those around you. By embracing a positive mindset, you align yourself with God's intentions for your life, opening the door to His abundant blessings and allowing His light to shine through you.

Months ago, I spent some quality time with a lady, sharing about our lives and how God's hand is fixing and moving things around us. She stated that she doesn't need a man because they have always used her and never appreciated her efforts. Instead, she was willing to devote all her time to God, as she had been doing for so long. While she was right about her past experiences, I realized that she was unhappy and living a life of denial. She denied herself many things that could have made her happy, unconsciously forcing herself to devote all her time to God without questioning if that was truly His plan for her. Clearly, she was not happy. What I want to emphasize here is that God did not create anyone to be miserable or unhappy. Often, we create a dark environment around ourselves through our thoughts and beliefs. We can even condemn ourselves for sins we think we have committed, without seeking God's perspective.

God's desire for us is to live a fulfilling and joyful life. By aligning our thoughts and actions with His will, we open ourselves to His blessings and guidance. Remember, God is the only one who can condemn you; you do not have the power to condemn yourself. Trust in His love and grace, and seek His will for your life, which includes happiness and fulfillment. It is important to reflect on whether our actions and sacrifices are truly in line with God's desires for us. Sometimes, in our quest for devotion, we might overlook the simple joys and blessings He wants us to experience. Living a balanced life, where we honor God and also embrace the good things He provides, is crucial for our spiritual and emotional well-being. God's plans for us are not meant to lead to a life of sorrow and deprivation. Instead, they are plans to prosper us, give us hope, and a future (Jeremiah 29:11). Embrace the life He has given you, and do not be afraid to seek happiness and fulfillment, knowing that this is also part of His divine plan for you.

Always remember that God created us to be happy, and everything in life has both a good side and a bad side. Take water, for example: it is essential for life, but too much water can cause devastating floods. Electricity brings light and powers our lives, yet a misuse of electricity can be fatal. Medicine can heal and save lives, but an overdose can be deadly. Skills and talents can improve and fix many things, but unethical use of these abilities can cause serious harm. This duality is a fundamental part of life. God has provided us with everything we need to live a fulfilling and joyful life. However, we often deny ourselves the very things that could bring us happiness. We sometimes focus too much on the potential negative outcomes and, in doing so, miss out on the blessings that God intends for us. God's gifts are meant to be used wisely and joyfully. He wants us to embrace the good things in life, while being mindful of their potential dangers. It's about finding balance and using discernment. Appreciate the positive aspects of what God has given us, and using them in ways that honor Him, we can experience true happiness.

Life is full of opportunities for joy and fulfillment. By aligning ourselves with God's will and being open to His blessings, we can fully enjoy the life He has planned for us. This means not only avoiding excess and misuse but also not shying away from the good things out of fear or guilt. God has equipped us with wisdom and discernment to navigate the complexities of life. Trusting in His guidance allows us to enjoy His creations responsibly and joyfully. It's about understanding that while every blessing comes with its own set of challenges, the intent is for us to thrive and live abundantly. In essence, God has given us everything we need to live life to the fullest. We must learn to embrace these gifts with gratitude, use them wisely, and allow ourselves to find joy in the life He has provided. By doing so, we honor God and fulfill the purpose for which we were created – to live in happiness and harmony with His creation.

## ❖ Embracing a life of faith and protection

Embracing a life of faith and protection begins with understanding that faith is more than just belief; it is a way of living that aligns every aspect of your life with God's will. Faith is the foundation upon which you build your relationship with God, trusting in His promises and His plan for your life. This trust provides a sense of security and peace, knowing that you are under His protection no matter what challenges you face. This relationship is nurtured through regular prayer, reading Scripture, and spending time in God's presence. Prayer is not just about asking for things but about communicating with God, sharing your heart, and listening for His guidance. Once clear and consistent communication with God is established, the blessings and benefits will begin to pour into your life in ways that may surprise you. The importance of maintaining an open line of communication with God cannot be overstated. It is through this ongoing dialogue that you build a deeper relationship with Him, one that transcends mere requests for material things. When you focus on truly communicating with God, sharing your heart, listening for His guidance, and expressing gratitude, you create a spiritual connection that brings profound peace and clarity. This connection helps you understand His will for your life and aligns your actions with His divine plan. It's not just about asking for things but about fostering a relationship built on trust, love, and mutual understanding. I cannot stress enough how crucial it is to prioritize this communication over simply asking for things. While it is natural to present your needs and desires to God, remember that a rich, fulfilling relationship with Him is built on more than just requests. It involves listening to His voice, seeking His wisdom, and allowing Him to shape your character and your path.

This spiritual intimacy brings about transformative changes. You may find that the things you once desperately sought are becoming less important as you grow closer to God and gain a deeper sense of His presence in your life. Your priorities will shift, and you will start to see what He desires for you, which often leads to greater fulfillment and joy. Moreover, this communication can strengthen your faith, providing you with the resilience and strength needed to face life's challenges. You will become more attuned to the ways in which God is working in your life, even in the smallest details, and this awareness brings immense comfort and encouragement. Prioritizing communication with God is to open yourself up to His endless grace and wisdom. The more you are engaged with Him, the more you will experience the fullness of His love and the richness of His blessings. So, make it a daily practice to spend quality time with God, not just asking for things but building a deep, meaningful relationship that will enrich every aspect of your life.

## ❖ Living in Obedience to God's Word

Living a life of faith means aligning your actions with God's commands and teachings. Obedience to God's Word is a key component of genuine faith, involving choices that reflect His will, even when those choices are difficult or counter to societal norms. This aspect of faith is both the most rewarding and the most challenging because, truthfully, we often struggle to listen and follow through. Choosing to live in obedience to God requires a deep commitment to His principles, often demanding that we go against the tide of popular opinion and cultural trends. It means prioritizing integrity, compassion, and righteousness over convenience and self-interest. This journey is not without its challenges, as our human nature and the world's pressures can make it difficult to stay true to God's path.

The rewards of living a life of faith are immeasurable. When we align our actions with God's commands, we experience a profound sense of peace and fulfillment that comes from knowing we are living according to His divine purpose. This alignment brings about spiritual growth, deeper relationships, and a clearer understanding of our place in God's grand design. The hard part, of course, is that we do not always listen. Distractions, temptations, and our own desires can lead us astray. Yet, it is in these moments of struggle that our faith is tested and strengthened. Embracing obedience to God's Word also means accepting that His ways are higher than ours. Trusting in His wisdom, even when it doesn't make sense to us, is a testament to our faith. It requires humility and a willingness to surrender our own plans in favor of His perfect plan. Do not be quick to blame yourself when you stumble while carrying your cross. Instead, seek to understand the reasons behind your fall and find ways to avoid similar pitfalls in the future, especially if the fall was unavoidable. Learn from the experience and use it as a stepping stone for growth. Remember, it's not about deliberately putting yourself in situations where you might falter. Self-compassion and proactive steps are essential in your journey of faith. Everyone encounters difficulties and setbacks; it is a natural part of the human experience. When you fall, it is an opportunity to reflect and grow stronger in your faith. Instead of succumbing to self-blame, turn to God for guidance and strength. He understands your struggles and is always ready to help you rise again. Seek His wisdom to navigate future challenges and to build resilience. It is important to recognize that falling is not the end of your journey but a moment to learn and adjust.

Evaluate the circumstances that led to your fall and identify practical steps to prevent it from happening again. This might involve setting stronger boundaries, seeking support from your faith community, or deepening your prayer and spiritual practices. My favorite thing is talking to the Lord. Speak to God, the King of Kings, and pour out your heart to Him. Explain your concerns, seek His guidance, and ask questions; He will answer in His perfect time. Do not weep in despair, for trust me, the devil is watching. When you talk to God with confidence, the devil trembles, but when you cry in hopelessness, he feels victorious. Don't let him win. Remember, God is aware of every challenge you face and allows them as tests to help us grow and draw closer to Him.

God sees everything that happens to us, and nothing catches Him by surprise. He uses these moments to refine us and strengthen our relationship with Him. It is through these trials that we learn to rely more on His wisdom and less on our own understanding. Trust that every test is designed to bring you closer to His divine presence and purpose for your life. In a future book, I will try to delve deeper into the journey of drawing closer to God. Indeed, it is a journey that is profoundly personal and often difficult to put into words. It requires patience, faith, and a willingness to seek His presence continually. As I seek more guidance from the Lord, I will begin writing about this spiritual journey. Not everything needs to be shared immediately; some truths may be challenging to accept and could potentially dishearten those who are not ready. The path to God requires spiritual maturity and openness to His guidance. Each person's journey is unique, and what might be a revelation to one could be overwhelming to another. Therefore, it is essential to approach this topic with sensitivity and discernment, ensuring that the message is received with the grace and intention it deserves.

Remember that in our walk with God, setbacks and trials are opportunities for growth. They are not signs of abandonment but rather invitations to deeper faith and trust. These moments of openly talking to God are incredibly powerful and transformative. Resist the devil's attempts to undermine your faith, as he will always try to do so. To be honest, you will encounter frustrations and disappointments, but always remember that these challenges are opportunities to elevate your spiritual life. Human beings are endowed with a wide range of emotions, and while these emotions are vital to our experiences, the devil often exploits them as weaknesses. Emotions guide us through our life cycle, enrich our experiences, and deeply connect us with others and with God. However, if not properly managed, they can also make us vulnerable to negative influences. The devil uses our emotions to sow doubt, fear, and despair, aiming to weaken our faith and disrupt our connection with God. Acknowledge and embrace your emotions while not letting them control and in moments of frustration and disappointment, turn to God and share your feelings with Him. Talk to Him and He will transform these emotions into a source of strength and resilience. God understands your struggles and provides the comfort and guidance needed to navigate through them. I know, I am somehow repeating myself, but it is very important that you understand this part as part of your stress comes from emotions. Each emotional challenge you face is an invitation to grow closer to God. These experiences test your faith, refine your character, and deepen your spiritual understanding. Instead of succumbing to the devil's manipulations, use these moments to strengthen your resolve and reinforce your trust in God's plan for your life. Live your life to the fullest.

### *Prayer to transform Emotion into source of strength and resilience*

*Heavenly Father, I come before You with a heart burdened by emotions that often overwhelm me. As Your Word promises in Psalm 34:17-18, "The righteous cry out, and the Lord hears them; He delivers them from all their troubles. The Lord is close to the brokenhearted and saves those who are crushed in spirit." I ask You, Lord, to transform these emotions into a source of strength and resilience. Turn my fears into courage, my sorrow into joy, and my anxiety into peace. Fill me with Your Holy Spirit, providing the comfort and strength I need to navigate through these feelings.*

*Lord, Your Word in Isaiah 41:10 reassures me, "So do not fear, for I am with you; do not be dismayed, for I am your God. I will strengthen you and help you; I will uphold you with my righteous right hand." Guide me through my emotional struggles and grant me clarity and understanding. Teach me to lean on You in moments of weakness and to draw from Your boundless grace. May my emotions be a testament to Your transformative power, showing others the strength that comes from a life fully surrendered to Your will.*

*Gracious God, I thank You for being my refuge and strength, as promised in Psalm 46:1, "God is our refuge and strength, an ever-present help in trouble." Surround me with Your comforting presence and help me find joy and peace in every circumstance. Strengthen my faith so that I can face each day with confidence and hope. I pray that my transformed emotions, guided by Your love, will lead me to a deeper relationship with You and a greater sense of purpose.*

___ ***In Jesus' name, I pray,***

___ ***Amen.***

# Conclusion

In the spiritual battle against the forces of evil, prayer is one of the most powerful weapons we possess. This book, 'I Will Pray for You: Breaking Free from the Devil's Influence,' aims to equip you with the knowledge and tools to recognize, resist, and overcome the negative influences that seek to undermine your faith and well-being. Through understanding the nature of spiritual warfare, the impact of curses, and the tactics used by the devil, you can fortify your spiritual defenses and live a life of freedom and victory. The concept of spiritual warfare may seem daunting, but it is a reality every believer must face. Spiritual warfare involves the battle between good and evil, light and darkness, where the devil seeks to disrupt God's plan for your life. Recognizing the signs of spiritual attacks such as persistent negative thoughts, unexplained difficulties, and a sense of oppression is the first step in protecting yourself. It is crucial to understand that the devil uses deception, temptation, and manipulation, tactics that are rarely taught in conventional settings. This knowledge is essential to better prepare you to resist his schemes.

The devil does not work alone; he employs agents to carry out his plans. These agents can be individuals who knowingly or unknowingly serve his purposes, spreading negativity and deceit. Understanding how these agents operate and recognizing their influence in your life is crucial. They may appear as friends, colleagues, or even family members who lead you away from God's truth. Staying vigilant and discerning, you can protect yourself from their harmful effects, but you might need to build a strong defense. Building a strong spiritual defense is not a passive endeavor. It requires active engagement with your faith through regular prayer, reading Scripture, and living in obedience to God's commandments. Prayer is your direct line of communication with God, where you seek His guidance, strength, and protection. Regularly reading the Bible fortifies your mind with God's truth, helping you to discern lies and deception. Obedience to God's Word aligns your actions with His will, creating a life that is resistant to the devil's influence.

Remember, you are not alone in this battle. Surrounding yourself with a supportive faith community provides strength, encouragement, and accountability. Being part of a church, prayer group, or fellowship helps you stay grounded in your faith and offers a network of support when you face spiritual challenges. Together, you can pray for one another, share experiences, and support each other in breaking free from the devil's influence.

Although I am not a big fan of fasting, prayer and fasting are powerful tools in spiritual warfare. Fasting helps you to focus on God by denying yourself physical sustenance, thereby heightening your spiritual awareness. Combined with prayer, fasting can break strongholds, deliver you from bondage, and bring about breakthroughs in areas where you have struggled. It is an act of humility and dependence on God, demonstrating your trust in His power to deliver and heal.

Try to live a life of obedience to God's Word as it is essential for spiritual health. This obedience involves making daily choices that reflect God's will, even when it is challenging or unpopular. It means prioritizing your relationship with God above all else and trusting that His ways are higher than yours. Obedience brings blessings and protection, shielding you from the devil's attempts to lead you astray. Breaking free from the devil's influence is not a one-time event but a continuous journey of spiritual growth. Regularly evaluate your spiritual health, seek God's guidance, and be willing to make necessary changes. Engage in lifelong learning through Bible study, attending faith-based seminars, and seeking mentorship from mature believers. Continuous growth strengthens your faith and equips you to face new challenges with confidence.

### *My Final Thoughts on Maintaining Vigilance and Faith*

Maintaining vigilance and faith in your spiritual journey is paramount. The devil's tactics are subtle and can easily lead you astray if you are not attentive. Regular prayer, immersion in Scripture, and a strong connection with your faith community are vital practices to stay grounded. Constantly seek God's guidance in all aspects of your life and remain aware of the spiritual battles around you. Faith is not just a passive belief but an active, living practice. Engage in daily conversations with God, expressing your fears, hopes, and gratitude. Faith is nurtured through trust in God's promises and reliance on His strength during trials. Remember that faith does not eliminate challenges but equips you to face them with resilience and hope. Your steadfast faith will be a beacon of light, guiding you through the darkest times and helping you emerge stronger and more committed to God's path.

Remember, as you continue your spiritual journey, seek God with all your heart. Understand that this journey is lifelong, filled with moments of growth, learning, and deepening your relationship with Him. Embrace each day as an opportunity to draw closer to God, to understand His will, and to live according to His purpose. Regularly set aside time for prayer, worship, and reflection, allowing God to speak to your heart and guide your steps. God desires for you to live a protected and prosperous life, not just materially, but spiritually and emotionally. Trust in His plan for you, even when the path seems unclear. Prosperity in God's terms encompasses peace, joy, and fulfillment that come from living a life aligned with His will. By prioritizing your relationship with God, you open yourself to His blessings and protection, experiencing the fullness of life He intends for you.

Live a protected and prosperous life by aligning your actions with God's commands and embracing His promises. Stay vigilant against spiritual attacks by continually fortifying your faith through prayer and Scripture. Engage in a community that supports your spiritual growth and holds you accountable. Remember, prosperity is not solely about material wealth but about a life rich in faith, love, and purpose. Trust in God's timing and wisdom, knowing that He works all things for your good. Face challenges with the assurance that God is with you, guiding and protecting you. Celebrate your victories, no matter how small, as evidence of God's faithfulness. By maintaining vigilance and unwavering faith, you not only protect yourself from the devil's schemes but also pave the way for a life filled with God's abundant blessings. Continue to seek Him diligently, and He will lead you into a life of peace, joy, and prosperity.

www.ingramcontent.com/pod-product-compliance
Lightning Source LLC
LaVergne TN
LVHW051051080426
835508LV00019B/1824